P9-DMP-497

Set Apart

Set Apart

Calling a
Worldly Church
to a
Godly Life

R. KENT HUGHES

CROSSWAY BOOKS

A PUBLISHING MINISTRY OF
GOOD NEWS PUBLISHERS
WHEATON, ILLINOIS

Set Apart

Copyright © 2003 by R. Kent Hughes

Published by Crossway Books
      a publishing ministry of Good News Publishers
      1300 Crescent Street
      Wheaton, Illinois 60187

All rights reserved. No part of this publication may be reproduced, stored in a retrieval system or transmitted in any form by any means, electronic, mechanical, photocopy, recording or otherwise, without the prior permission of the publisher, except as provided by USA copyright law.

Cover design: Josh Dennis

Cover photo: Getty Images

First printing, 2003

Printed in the United States of America

Unless otherwise indicated, Scripture quotations are from *The Holy Bible: English Standard Version*®, copyright © 2001 by Crossway Bibles, a publishing ministry of Good News Publishers. Used by permission. All rights reserved.

Scripture quotations indicated NASB are taken from the *New American Standard Bible,* copyright © 1960, 1962, 1963, 1968, 1971, 1972, 1973, 1975, 1977, 1995 by the Lockman Foundation.

Library of Congress Cataloging-in-Publication Data
Hughes, R. Kent
   Set apart : calling a worldly church to a godly life / R. Kent Hughes.
     p. cm.
   ISBN 13: 978-1-58134-491-2 (trade pbk.)
   ISBN 10: 1-58134-491-0
   1. Church renewal—United States. 2. Christianity and culture—United States. 3. Church and social problems—United States. 4. Church and the world. 5. United States—Moral conditions. 6. Evangelicalism—United States. I. Title.
BV600.3.H84   2003
262'.001'7—dc21   2003000053

BP		17	16	15	14	13	12	11	10	09	08	07
15	14	13	12	11	10	9	8	7	6	5	4	3

For my wife, Barbara,
whose encouragement and convictions
inspire me

Table of Contents

Acknowledgments

Anyone who writes theology is aware of standing on the shoulders of past saints. And when it is done in the week-in, week-out hustle and bustle of the church "with all the saints" (Ephesians 3:18), those who write know that what they have accomplished comes from the saints' locking their arms in prayer and advice. Here I must give thanks for the strong arms of College Church elders Roger Sandberg, Harold Smith, Wayne Martindale, and Lee Ryken for their advice and their weekly leading the congregation in discussion of the issues. I must especially thank Dr. Ryken for his masterful editing of the manuscript before it arrived in the capable hands of Crossway Books Managing Editor, Ted Griffin. And, as always during the past fifteen years, my ongoing thanks goes to my Administrative Assistant, Sharon Fritz for preparing the manuscript, and to Herb Carlburg for weekly proofing. Of course, my deepest thanks goes to my wife, Barbara, for her intense interest, advice, and prayers.

Preface

The chapters of this book were originally a series of sermons that I preached. The series was partly occasioned by a convergence of my preaching on Lot's lamentable accommodations to Sin City (Genesis 19) and my reading of Robert Gundry's book *Jesus the Word According to John the Sectarian*, which offered a critique of contemporary evangelicalism. I eventually added to Gundry's list of ailments afflicting evangelical churches today. I will note in passing that my church devoted the Sunday evenings during the series to question-and-answer sessions on the topic on which I had preached in the morning.

Part of my venture can be called cultural critique, by which I mean that I begin my chapters with a survey of sociological data that delineates where our culture and the church stand on the announced topic. Not everyone is comfortable with such cultural critique from the pulpit. In one of the evening question-and-answer sessions, someone submitted a note saying that I should stop talking about culture and just preach the Gospel.

I understand the impulse behind that comment. A sermon that gives extensive initial attention to sociological data and cultural analysis has a different feel from a sermon that single-mindedly works its way through a biblical passage. But there is a time and place for cultural critique among Christians. Our own time and place require that we take stock of what is actually happening in our culture and in the church. The evidence is pretty clear that we do not understand either of these as well as we should. Among evangelicals, there is a great disconnect between (on the one hand) what Christians believe and assimilate from sermons and Christian sources and how (on the other hand) they actually live. It is this very disconnect that is the subject of this book.

The model for cultural critique as part of the religious life exists within the Bible itself. The Old Testament prophets were thoroughgoing cultural critics. They did not simply preach a remedy for cultural ills; they took the time to portray the cultural situation to which they offered solutions. The resulting prophetic discourse as we find it in the Old Testament combines (sometimes shocking) exposés with exhortations about what God requires of his people.

In the New Testament, Jesus and the apostolic writers of the epistles do exactly the same thing. Jesus repeatedly mingles analysis of what was awry in his own social world with his teaching about the godly life. As for the New Testament epistles, there is so much reference to problems in the early church in its cultural setting that a main difficulty we have as modern readers is to work through the mass of cultural references en route to discovering the moral and spiritual application to our own lives.

The contemporary evangelical church is not lacking for moral and spiritual instruction. It *is* lacking in its ability to remain uncontaminated by the unchristian thinking and morality of contemporary culture. It is doubtless true that there has been too much cultural criticism and not enough gospel content in theological liberalism. But in contemporary evangelicalism there has been a deficiency of cultural awareness and a resulting lack of discernment regarding how the world has overwhelmed the thinking and behavior of Christians. This book is my contribution to the attempt to correct the imbalance.

For those who wish to engage in personal thought on each chapter, or who wish to use this book as a springboard to group discussion, here is a basic grid of questions for each chapter. These questions may be used in place of, or to augment, the specific discussion questions listed at the end of each chapter.

• What experiences and observations can you supply to confirm and illustrate the claims made in this chapter regarding cultural trends?

• Have you observed inroads that these cultural trends have made in the church or in your personal life?

• What (if anything) in the survey of cultural trends or the life of the church surprised or shocked you?

• What did you personally find most convicting in this chapter?

• What general themes or specific details in the survey of biblical material stands out to you as being the most important?

• What are the most obvious applications that you can make on the basis of this chapter in your personal life or in the life of your church?

1

Set Apart to Save

"Now therefore, if you will indeed obey my voice and keep my covenant, you shall be my treasured possession among all peoples, for all the earth is mine; and you shall be to me a kingdom of priests and a holy nation. These are the words that you shall speak to the people of Israel."

EXODUS 19:5-6

As you come to him, a living stone rejected by men but in the sight of God chosen and precious, you yourselves like living stones are being built up as a spiritual house, to be a holy priesthood, to offer spiritual sacrifices acceptable to God through Jesus Christ.

1 PETER 2:4-5

If we had only the story of Lot's life as it is told in the book of Genesis, we would never have imagined that Lot was a true believer. But Second Peter 2 tells us three times that this conflicted, compromised man was "righteous"—and more, that he was "distressed" and tormented by life in Sodom. Peter's carefully crafted description of Lot is this: ". . . righteous Lot, greatly distressed by the sensual conduct of the wicked (for as that righteous man lived among them day after day, he was tormenting his righteous soul over their lawless deeds that he saw and heard) . . ." (vv. 7-8). Ironically, though Lot was revolted by Sodom, Sodom was in his soul. It is possible, then, for a believer to be distressed by the world while willfully clinging to the world.

There is every evidence that righteous Lot was of no benefit whatsoever to the inhabitants of Sodom. Though he lived in Sodom for years and was prominent in its gates, and therefore would have had many opportunities to influence his friends, Lot utterly disappointed. When judgment fell on Sodom, not one righteous person could be found outside his family. No acquaintances, no neighbors, not one of his servants had come to know the Lord. His plea with the Sodomites in front of his door was dismissed by them out of hand. Lot lacked *gravitas*; his words carried no weight.

Even more tragically, Lot's life did nothing to point his family and relatives to heaven. None of his family or friends feared God. When he urged his then future sons-in-law to flee the cities' destruction, they thought he was "jesting." Lot's words had no substance because *he* was so insubstantial. Additionally Lot's lifestyle had done nothing to loosen the culture's grip on his wife. She left her heart in Sodom and therefore couldn't resist turning around—to her destruction. The very woman who bore his children, who was on most intimate terms with him, who knew the contours of his soul, saw nothing in him or in his faith to point her from earth to heaven.

It is also evident that Lot's life choices had promoted his daughters' absorbing of the spirit of Sodom into their souls. Deception, of course, was a way of life in Sodom. And Lot was part of it. But his deception was spiritually charged and therefore domestically lethal. Inwardly he was "greatly distressed by the sensual conduct of the wicked" and "was tormenting his righteous soul," says Peter; but outwardly he said little or nothing because he had become a prominent man in town. Forthrightness, anything approaching a witness, would have jeopardized his standing. Lot had mastered the craft of turning a blind eye and deaf ear to the social and sexual abuses of Sodom. He didn't *practice* them. He didn't *approve* of them. He *loathed* them. But he didn't speak out against them. Blasphemies and filthy speech were met by Lot's easy politic smile and careful deflection.

His daughters saw his accommodating character that so deftly masked what he really thought. Lot the survivor was a master. His girls could not forget that he had offered them to appease the inflamed men of Sodom in his infamous betrayal of fatherly duty. So when the successive father-daughter seductions took place, his girls used the craft he had bequeathed to them. It was *his* wine, *his* deceit, *his* betrayal mixed together and served in a dark cup in the depths of the cave. His daughters' dishonor of him was brilliant, because with cruel irony he himself carried out the shameful act he had first suggested to the men of Sodom. Lot had effectively sown Sodom into his daughters' souls.

Lot's folly was this: Though the worldliness of Sodom vexed his righteous soul, he lived as close to the world as he could, hanging on to it for dear life until the bitter end. And the result was that though God judged all of Sodom except Lot and his daughters, *Sodom was reborn* in their very lives. We see, then, that it is possible for believing people like us who are truly distressed by the course of this world to live lives that are so profoundly influenced by culture that Sodom is reborn in the lives of those we love the most.

Fair warnings. The enticements to yield to this syndrome and become indistinct from culture have never been more powerful than they are right now because of our prosperity, cyber-options, and the powers of the media. I sense that these are crucial days culturally and spiritually. And I am not alone. Those who poll religious interests— including George Gallup, Barna Research, the Princeton Religion Research Center, and ChristianityToday.com—indicate that evangelical Christianity is becoming increasingly worldly, and that it is ever more becoming a mere mirror of secular culture.

The September 2001 issue of *Emerging Trends*, published by the Princeton Religion Research Center, bears the headline "Religion Is Gaining Ground, But Morality Is Losing Ground." Positively it notes that adult weekly church attendance has increased from 38 percent in 1996 to 44 percent in 2000—up 6 percent in four years. The same is true of teenaged students, only higher, from 42 percent to 53 percent, an increase of 11 percent in four years. There is also an uptrend in adult Bible reading (weekly or two or three times weekly), from 18 percent in 1982 to 26 percent in 2000. Yet at the same time one Gallup Poll indicates that 78 percent say that our moral values are "somewhat weak" or "very weak" and that morals are in decline.[1]

This is corroborated by a study by the Evangelical Alliance (the British counterpart to the National Association of Evangelicals), which found that one third of evangelicals between the ages of eighteen and thirty-five say they have no problem with unmarried men and women living together.[2] One Christian college president here in the U.S. confided to a *Christianity Today* editor that the most perplexing puzzle he and his staff were facing regarding their present student body was that student leaders were outspoken in their Christian commitment and yet living with a girlfriend or boyfriend—and not seeing a disconnect.[3] Significantly, Barna Research listed the following as one of the most discouraging findings of 2000: "Born again adults are more likely to experience a divorce than are non-born again adults (27% vs. 24%)."[4]

In the same issue it was noted that a minority of born-again adults (44 percent) and an even smaller proportion of born-again teenagers (9 percent) are certain of the existence of absolute moral truth.[5] George Barna's recent book *Boiling Point* categorically states that moral anarchy has arrived and rules our culture, and that we are now in a state of spiritual anarchy.[6] The implication is that some ominous times are ahead for a church that dares to insist that there is absolute truth. This isn't helped by the biblical ignorance that afflicts so many young Christians in the upcoming generation, 40 percent of whom hold the view that Jesus Christ committed sins![7]

All of this together—the ignorance, the spiritual anarchy, the growing acceptance of relativism among Christians, divorce rates that exceed those of secular culture, the rise of cohabitation among professing Christians, the increase of worldliness in the church despite growing attendance and Bible reading—suggests that the church is becoming indistinct from the world—*worldly*. And more, the failure of its increasing numbers to make a difference in the world shouts of compromise. Indeed, what we see now may be an Indian summer, the last gasp of the warm, sunny days before a long, dark spiritual winter.

Who can deny Robert Gundry's assertion that the evangelical enterprise has become worldly, that materialism grips the church, that pleasure-seeking dominates us, that evangelicals watch sensuality and violence like everyone else, that immodesty is *de jure*, that voyeurism and pornography and sexual laxity and divorce are on the rise, and that we, like Lot, could find that Sodom has been born anew in our own homes. God help us if while decrying sin, we are sprinting headlong after it.

We must lay this to heart: A worldly church cannot and will not reach the world. The church must be distinct from the world to reach the world. We must set ourselves apart to God if we hope to reach the world. In a word, the only hope for us and the lost world is a holy church.

GOD'S PLAN: A PEOPLE SET APART (DISTINCT) FROM THE WORLD TO REACH THE WORLD

From the onset God's plan for reaching the world has been to create a people distinct from the world who would then minister to and reach the world.

God's plan: Israel. This was God's global plan for his chosen people as first told to Abraham: "And I will make of you a great nation, and I will bless you . . . and in you all the families of the earth shall be blessed" (Genesis 12:2-3; cf. 18:18).

A kingdom of priests. As Israel became a nation during the four centuries that followed their captivity in Egypt, the manner of their becoming a blessing was unclear. But after the Exodus and before Israel's entry into the Promised Land, God made it very clear to Moses as he gave them the Ten Commandments: "You yourselves have seen what I did to the Egyptians, and how I bore you on eagles' wings and brought you to myself. Now therefore, if you will indeed obey my voice and keep my covenant, you shall be my treasured possession among all peoples, for all the earth is mine; and you shall be to me a kingdom of priests and a holy nation" (Exodus 19:4-6). As a kingdom of priests they would then offer sacrifices and intercede for the whole world. What a stupendous designation—a kingdom of priests—every Israelite a priest to the Gentile nations!

A holy people. The key, the secret, behind Israel's worldwide ministry was to be their holiness (or set-apartness) as a holy nation. The parallel version of their commission at Mount Sinai in Deuteronomy says, "For you are a people holy to the LORD your God. The LORD your God has chosen you to be a people for his treasured possession" (Deuteronomy 7:6). Holiness is essential to God's nature; it is not so much an attribute of God as it is the very foundation of his being. Holiness denotes the separateness or otherness of God from all his creation. God is set apart from all that is unclean or evil.

The holiness of God was to be the example and motivation for God's people to be set apart as holy, that they might reach the world. This is a great theme in the book of Leviticus, which repeatedly highlights the fact that they must be distinct from and holier than the nations around them:

> *"For I am the LORD who brought you up out of the land of Egypt to be your God. You shall therefore be holy, for I am holy."*
>
> —LEVITICUS 11:45

> *And the LORD spoke to Moses, saying, "Speak to all the congregation of the people of Israel and say to them, You shall be holy, for I the LORD your God am holy."*
>
> —LEVITICUS 19:1-2

> *"Consecrate yourselves, therefore, and be holy, for I am the LORD your God. Keep my statutes and do them; I am the LORD who sanctifies you."*
>
> —LEVITICUS 20:7-8

> *"You shall be holy to me, for I the LORD am holy and have separated you from the peoples, that you should be mine."*
>
> —LEVITICUS 20:26

The sum of their call was that they be separated to God and consecrated to serve him in holiness. This is where their power lay. Israel's distinctiveness was to leverage them for ministry to a sinful world.

A light to the Gentiles. Isaiah repeatedly refers to Israel as a light for the Gentiles. The context of those declarations is the servant songs in which the servant is sometimes corporate Israel and sometimes an individual servant, prophesying the Messiah, the ultimate light to the Gentiles (see 42:6; 49:1-6; cf. 60:1). But national Israel, set apart as holy, was in its time to be a beacon to the dark Gentile world.

But Israel never reached its potential. Aaron's golden calf shows how miserably Israel could fail in becoming a nation holy to the Lord (cf. Exodus 32—34). Likewise, the failed attempt to enter Canaan was due to Israel's faithlessness and fears (cf. Numbers 13—14). Israel's repeated lapses into idolatry as recorded in Judges, the sins of the latter prophets, and the many failures of the people all testify to their descent from holiness, despite glowing exceptions. Israel never achieved its potential as a kingdom of priests and a light to the Gentiles.

Someday, as Zechariah says:

> *"Many peoples and strong nations shall come to seek the LORD of hosts in Jerusalem and to entreat the favor of the LORD. Thus says the LORD of hosts: In those days ten men from the nations of every tongue shall take hold of the robe of a Jew, saying, 'Let us go with you, for we have heard that God is with you.'"*
>
> —ZECHARIAH 8:22-23

But that did not happen with national Israel. It yet awaits a future fulfillment in the last days.

God's plan: Jesus. When Jesus came, he succeeded where Israel had failed. As the ultimate seed of Abraham, Jesus is true Israel (cf. Galatians 3:16). He was called out of Egypt as was the nation of Israel (cf. Matthew 2:15). As true Israel, he succeeded in resisting Satan's wilderness temptations, whereas corporate Israel had failed (cf. Matthew 4:1-11; Luke 4:1-13). Jesus was at once set apart as holy to God the Father, a great high priest and a light to the Gentiles.

• *Holy:* Jesus was the Holy One of God (cf. Mark 1:24; John 6:69). He had set himself apart as holy, praying on the very night of his death, "And for their sake I consecrate myself, that they also may be sanctified in truth" (John 17:19). Holiness was the province of Jesus' soul.

• *Priest*: At his ascension Jesus became a high priest in the order of Melchizedek who eternally and tirelessly intercedes for his people (Hebrews 7).

• *Light*: After Jesus' birth, when his parents brought him to the temple, aged Simeon swept up Jesus in his arms and sang:

> *"Lord, now you are letting your servant depart in peace,*
> *according to your word;*
> *for my eyes have seen your salvation*
> *that you have prepared in the presence of all peoples,*
> *a light for revelation to the Gentiles,*
> *and for glory to your people Israel."*
>
> —LUKE 2:29-32

Thirty-three years later in the same temple, Jesus declared, "I am the light of the world. Whoever follows me will not walk in darkness, but will have the light of life" (John 8:12).

God's plan: the church. Today the threefold responsibility that was corporate Israel's—and that of Jesus, the true Israel—falls to the church. The apostle Peter, in chapter 2 of his first letter, refers to Exodus 19:6 (where Israel had been first called to be a kingdom of priests) by telling believers that they themselves are now a holy priesthood: "As you come to him, a living stone rejected by men but in the sight of God chosen and precious, you yourselves like living stones are being built up as a spiritual house, to be a holy priesthood, to offer spiritual sacrifices acceptable to God through Jesus Christ" (1 Peter 2:4-5). Again, "But you are a chosen race, a royal priesthood, a holy nation, a people for his own possession, that you may proclaim the excellencies of him who called you out of darkness into his marvelous light" (v. 9). We are all to declare that Christ is the light of the world, both Jews and Gentiles.

As to our holiness, the Scriptures declare that we are both "sanctified in Christ Jesus, called to be saints [holy]" (1 Corinthians 1:2).

This verse contains the *indicative* of what we are ("sanctified," i.e., holy) and the *imperative* of what we are to be ("saints [or holy]," i.e., sanctified). Thus we *are* holy and must *become* holy!

We are sanctified (set apart as holy) because Jesus is "our righteousness and sanctification and redemption" (1 Corinthians 1:30). Fifty-six times the New Testament designates believers as *saints* (holy ones). The common compliment, "she's a real saint," referring to a woman's goodness, is nice but uninformed. All believers are real saints (cf. Romans 1:7; 1 Corinthians 1:2; 2 Corinthians 1:1; Ephesians 1:1; Philippians 1:1; Colossians 1:2).

And here lies our great advantage as believers. The call to be holy is not a call to a bootstrap moralistic improvement. Rather, it is a call to live out the practical implications of our holiness in Christ by pursuing holiness as a lifestyle. Our renewal and change flow from the sanctification that God has already accomplished in our lives. As "holy and beloved" by God, we are to abandon the values and attitudes and practices that belong to the old self and be clothed with the new self (cf. Colossians 3:9-10, 12). We are to live with a confidence in what God has already done for us and to trust in him to continue his transforming work until we see him face to face.

> *Finish then Thy new creation,*
> *Pure and spotless let us be;*
> *Let us see Thy great salvation*
> *Perfectly restored in Thee.*
> *Changed from glory into glory,*
> *Till in heav'n we take our place,*
> *Till we cast our crowns before Thee,*
> *Lost in wonder, love, and praise.*
>
> CHARLES WESLEY, 1747

HOW TO BE SET APART

Still, while holy living is not a matter of moralistic self-improvement, and while it is allowing what already has taken place to renew our lives, it remains a daunting task. It requires saying no to our sinful desires. It requires discipline. It requires prayer and vigilance.

The stakes are so high. Righteous Lot loved Sodom. While scandalized by it, he hung on to it for dear life. And he and his family paid dearly. So listen carefully. Setting ourselves apart from the world so that we might reach the world is not so much a series of noes as much as it is an immense yes to Christ and all that he gives. A great yes to the riches of Christ supplies the perspective to say no when and as we ought. When we say yes to Christ, we say yes to eternal salvation. (For a clear explanation of the Gospel from the Old and New Testaments, see Appendix I: "The Gospel—Old and New.") We say yes to a love that is a shoreless, bottomless sea. We say yes to the endless Niagara Falls of grace so that no matter how much we have received, there always is more grace (John 1:16; James 4:6). We say yes to the indwelling of Christ (2 Corinthians 5:17). We say yes to becoming a temple of him who is the eternal temple (1 Corinthians 3:16; 6:19). We say yes to light that fills us now and is eternal (Matthew 5:14-16). We say yes to God's care that is ministered in the full orbs of his omnipresence, omnipotence, and omniscience (Psalm 139). We say yes to citizenship in heaven, and we are *now* seated in Christ in the heavenly places because Christ is in heaven and we are in him (Ephesians 2:6). We say yes to heaven and the new Jerusalem coming down from heaven like a bride beautifully dressed for her husband (Revelation 21:1-2). And we say yes to his Lordship over all of life (Romans 12:1-2). His sovereignty commands every area of life. This yes is the sweetest of all—and the key to the noes he calls us to declare.

The stakes are indeed high. Lot's folly could be ours. We are more than capable of being tormented in our righteous souls by the deeds of lawless men, all the while hanging on to the same world with all we have, so that Sodom is reborn in the lives of our nearest and dearest.

God help us.

NOTES

1. *Emerging Trends,* September 2001, Vol. 23, No. 7, The Princeton Religion Research Center, pp. 1-2.
2. ChristianityToday.com—*LeadershipJournal*.net-6, "Trends Facing Christians," p. 2.
3. Personal conversation with Harold Smith, editor for CTi.
4. Barna Research Online, "The Year's Most Intriguing Findings." From Barna Research Studies, December 12, 2001.
5. Ibid.
6. Barna Research Online, "Researcher Predicts Mounting Challenges to Christian Church," April 16, 2001.
7. Barna Research Online, "Teenagers' Beliefs Moving Further from Biblical Perspectives," October 23, 2000.

2

Set Apart to Save:
Materialism

And he said to them, "Take care, and be on your guard against all covetousness, for one's life does not consist in the abundance of his possessions." And he told them a parable, saying, "The land of a rich man produced plentifully, and he thought to himself, 'What shall I do, for I have nowhere to store my crops?' And he said, 'I will do this: I will tear down my barns and build larger ones, and there I will store all my grain and my goods. And I will say to my soul, Soul, you have ample goods laid up for many years; relax, eat, drink, be merry.' But God said to him, 'Fool! This night your soul is required of you, and the things you have prepared, whose will they be?' So is the one who lays up treasure for himself and is not rich toward God."

LUKE 12:15-21

The final decades of the twentieth century saw an almost exponential rise in consumerism as represented by credit card spending. In 1970, Americans owed five billion dollars in credit card debt. But twenty-five years later in 1995, the total credit card debt had risen to 395 billion dollars, an increase of 2,000 percent. The debt curve had become almost vertical. Just two years later, in 1997, credit card debt had risen by sixty billion dollars to an estimated 455 billion dollars. Today the average balance on a credit card is seven thousand dollars, and the average interest rate is 18.9 percent. The average American household has ten credit cards. Statistics indicate that credit card companies solicit the average American seven times a year through the mail. My experience is that this is a far too conservative estimate—that it's more like seven times a month. And that doesn't include phone solicitation. Typically, usurious credit card interest can lead to decades of long enslavement. A modest fifteen thousand dollars at 14.99 percent interest will take 222 months or eighteen and a half years to pay off with the minimum payment of two hundred dollars per month—provided you don't charge anything else.

In 2002 Americans paid out approximately sixty-five billion dollars in credit card interest alone.[1] This doesn't include interest on home mortgages, car loans, student loans, or utilities and telephones. Americans are consumerist to the core. And if I have heard the President correctly, good Americans should go out and spend more money to get the economy going. It's our patriotic duty! The truth is, we are consumerist by nature. Consumerism is universal and timeless.

But never has consumerism been promoted with such premeditation and art. In 1955 retailing analyst Victor Lebow declared, "Our enormously productive economy . . . demands that we make consumption our way of life, that we convert the buying and use of goods into rituals, that we seek our spiritual satisfaction, our ego satisfaction, in consumption. . . . We need things consumed, burned up, worn out, replaced, and discarded at an ever increasing rate."[2] Every syllable of Victor Lebow's oracle has come true. The very way we express ourselves demonstrates that consumerism has become a way of life. As Rodney Clapp so well stated in his *Christianity Today* essay "Why the Devil Takes Visa":

> In the language of marketers, people who go to movies are not "audiences," but "consumers"; those who go to school are no longer "students," but "educational consumers." People who visit a physician are no longer "patients," those who go to church are no longer "worshipers," those who go to libraries and bookstores are no longer "readers," those who go to restaurants are no longer "diners." All are as frequently designated "consumers."[3]

Consumerist materialism has insinuated itself into our souls with a metaphysical power that in effect doubts Paul's assertion that "the things that are seen are transient, but the things that are unseen are eternal" (2 Corinthians 4:18). And more, because we're so immersed in materialism, we cannot see it for what it is. John Stott once said that our blindness to materialism is similar to the western culture's blindness to the sins of slavery in the eighteenth and nineteenth centuries. Today we look back in amazement that Christian people could not see it for the evil it was. And likely, thinks Stott, future generations, should they look back, will regard our day with the same perplexity: *How could they not have seen it?*

Christians cannot exempt themselves from the general culture of materialism. The statistics will not allow us, because the spending habits of most Christians are indistinguishable from those of other Americans. Do we give? On the average it isn't much—less than 3 percent. Tellingly, only 8 percent of born-again Christian adults tithe their income to their church.[4] Christians spend seven times more on entertainment than they do on spiritual activities.[5]

Setting ourselves apart from materialism has everything to do with the spread of the Gospel among the nations. We cannot be *like* the nations and at the same time a *light to* the nations. A worldly church will not reach the world. If our materialistic pursuits are no different from those of general culture, we will have little to say to culture. If the Gospel has not set us free from the gravity of materialism, if we do not soar above the culture of materialism, what can we have to say to the earthbound people of this world? If we live for the things of Sodom, how will we point others to the hills of salvation?

Don't misunderstand. Our holiness, our being set apart from materialism, will not save anyone. Only Christ does that. The church's job is not to save culture but to rescue the perishing. But at the same time, as we truly set our hearts on things above, where Christ is seated at the right hand of God, and not on earthly things, God will be pleased to use us to point others to him.

THE BIBLE ON WEALTH

Not long ago a pastor in a well-known church preached on money, which prompted this anonymous letter:

> I was never so disappointed in a service as I was Sunday. I have an unbelieving friend that I got to come with me, and what were you preaching about? *Money!* I can assure you she was not impressed! And why money, when there are so many beautiful things to say? You'd better reconsider such messages in the future. Leave money to God, and he will handle everything, believe me. I love this church and usually like the sermons, but that was terrible.

The letter was signed, "A Christian who loves to go to church to hear the Word."[6] Well, the fact that the sermon was an excellent exposition of the Word and that many others had a positive response to the sermon makes the parting shot dubious. Perhaps it should have more accurately read, "A Christian who loves to go to church to hear the Word as long as it doesn't focus on such sensitive subjects as money. Leave the money to God, and I will feel so much better." Such thinking is also ignorant of the fact that 450 separate biblical passages deal with wealth, and that money is the second most dominant motif in the Bible, following idolatry. You cannot faithfully preach the Word without addressing the subject of money.

Tellingly, Jesus Christ, God Incarnate, spoke more about money than about heaven or hell, and nowhere is this more evident than in the Gospel of Luke. The context into which Jesus came was humble. His mother glorified the Lord because he had "looked on the humble estate of his servant" (Luke 1:48). When Christ was born, the event was first announced to a despised class of humble means—"shepherds, . . . keeping watch over their flock by night" (2:8). And when baby Jesus was taken to be presented in the temple, he was greeted and celebrated by Simeon and Anna, humble-living representatives of the righteous remnant who were longing for Messiah (2:25ff.).

The very first recorded words of Jesus' public ministry were quoted from Isaiah 61:1-2: "The Spirit of the Lord is upon me, because he has anointed me to proclaim good news to the poor" (Luke 4:18)—those conscious of their moral and spiritual poverty, which is often the lot of the financially poor.

Jesus next referenced this same group in Luke 6:20 when he said, "Blessed are you who are poor, for yours is the kingdom of God," and then in verse 24, "But woe to you who are rich, for you have received your consolation." Clearly Jesus viewed wealth as a spiritual disadvantage because of the pride and self-sufficiency it engenders.

Then in Luke 12:15-21 Jesus delivered the parable of the rich fool who died the very night he contemplated his bulging barns. The story illustrated Jesus' warning to the rich: "Take care, and be on your guard against all covetousness, for one's life does not consist in the abundance of his possessions" (v. 15).

In the parable of the shrewd manager, Jesus first advised, "And I tell you, make friends for yourselves by means of unrighteous wealth, so that when it fails they may receive you into the eternal dwellings" (Luke 16:9). Believers are to use their wealth and possessions to win eternal friends who, should they precede their benefactors to heaven, will welcome them when they arrive. This is the divinely recommended use of wealth.

Jesus closed that same parable with this famous warning: "No servant can serve two masters, for either he will hate the one and love the other, or he will be devoted to the one and despise the other. You cannot serve God and money" (Luke 16:13). This is radical. There is no middle ground. If we are devoted to money, we will "despise" God with our intellect and "hate" him with our emotions and the totality of our being.

Luke 16 closes with the parable of the beggar Lazarus and the ungenerous rich man who at death discover a mighty reversal that left Lazarus in Abraham's bosom and the rich man in hell, begging Abraham for relief. "But Abraham said, 'Child, remember that you in your lifetime received your good things, and Lazarus in like manner bad things; but now he is comforted here, and you are in anguish'" (v. 25).

Next, in Luke 18, when a rich man balked at Jesus' challenge to
give his possessions to the poor and follow him, Jesus responded,
"How difficult it is for those who have wealth to enter the kingdom
of God! For it is easier for a camel to go through the eye of a needle
than for a rich person to enter the kingdom of God" (vv. 24b-25)—
stating categorically, therefore, that it is impossible for a man or
woman who *trusts* in riches to get into heaven. There is, then, a proper
fear of being rich. There are disadvantages to having wealth—primarily what it can do to your soul.

Lastly, there is the salvation of a rich little man named
Zacchaeus, a man who was filthy rich in the literal sense of the
term, having made his money by exacting Rome's taxes from his
countrymen. Amazingly, when rich Zacchaeus came to Christ, he
gave half his possessions to the poor and fourfold reparations to
anyone he had cheated. The impossible had happened to camel-
brained, dromedary-souled Zacchaeus. The kingpin of the Jericho
tax cartel had miraculously passed through the eye of a needle
because of the grace of God. And Jesus declared, "Today salvation
has come to this house, since he also is a son of Abraham. For
the Son of Man came to seek and to save the lost" (19:9-10).
Zacchaeus' newly found generosity was concomitant with his saving faith.

From beginning to end, Luke's theology (quoting the words of
Jesus) views wealth as a spiritual handicap. His "woe" to the rich, his
parable of the rich fool, his epigram "you cannot serve God and
money," his parable of Lazarus and the rich man, his declaration that
it is easier for a camel to pass through the eye of a needle than for a
rich man to get into heaven, and finally the salvation of rich
Zacchaeus who responded by divesting himself of his riches—all testify that material wealth is a spiritual hindrance. The evidence is that
every time Jesus offers an opinion about riches, it is negative. Each
time he teaches on wealth, he advises giving it away.[7] For those of us
who take the Bible seriously, this raises great tensions—sanctifying
tensions.

THE BENEFITS OF WEALTH

The fact that wealth is a spiritual danger in no way suggests that money is evil. Many of the Old Testament greats were well-heeled, including Abraham, Job, David, and Solomon. And the same was true of some of Jesus' followers, such as Lazarus and his sisters Mary and Martha, Nicodemus, Joseph of Arimathea, and Zacchaeus. Jesus' ministry was supported by wealthy women (cf. Luke 8:2-3).

Paul set the record straight in his explanation to Timothy: "For the love of money is a root of all kinds of evils" (1 Timothy 6:10). Randy Alcorn summarizes, "Money makes a good servant to those who have the right master, but it makes a terrible master itself. . . . Money may be temporarily under my control. But I must always regard it as a wild beast, with power to turn on me and others if I drop my guard."[8]

Among the universal benefits of money is that you don't have to sweat the "small stuff." Money takes care of car repairs, mowing the lawn, cleaning the house, and paying bills. It provides substantial physical comforts and can buy the best care and education. And it can provide huge spiritual benefits. The independence that comes with old money, for example, is time for ministry. And it is a beautiful thing when people use their wealth in this way.

Possessions, large homes, recreational capacities, and estates have enabled huge ministry. Allan Emery, one of the founding partners of ServiceMaster, said that possessions become either idols or tools.[9] And he has used his immense wealth as a tool to serve God, under-writing hundreds at ministries and repeatedly refreshing the saints. A. W. Tozer, in a remarkable essay entitled "The Transmutation of Wealth," put it this way: "Any temporal possession can be turned into everlasting wealth. Whatever is given to Christ is immediately touched with immortality."[10]

THE DANGERS OF WEALTH

The downside of wealth is well-documented. It can be delusive, idolatrous, and damning.

Delusive. Wealth is intrinsically delusive. Wealth deludes people into imagining that they are of superior value—"I have more money than other people—therefore I am better. And certainly God recognizes my superiority—otherwise I would not be so blessed." Of course a Mafia don can use the same reasoning. But no matter. Riches can delude us into imagining that moral superiority is a matter of homes and cars and yachts and designer labels. Timex and Rolex both end in *ex*, but the wearer of one can imagine a universe of superiority above the other. Wealth can create an illusion of character and originality. It can even make you imagine that you are charming, because it can buy hearers who will laugh at your jokes. Wealthy men, especially, seem readily deluded into thinking that because the public defers to wealth, they have the answer for everything—politics, theology, child-rearing, global warming, and much more.

Idolatrous. Though money is neutral in itself, if your heart is not devoted to God, it can take on what Philip Yancey describes as "an irrational, almost magical power. . . . It is a force with a personality. It is in truth, a god, and Jesus called it that."[11]

Damning. And, of course, the delusive, idolatrous powers of wealth intensify its capability to damn the soul. The deceitfulness of riches chokes out the Word (Mark 4:19). The god of riches instills pride and independence and anesthetizes the victim so that he or she feels no need. As Jesus charged the lukewarm church of Laodicea, "For you say, I am rich, I have prospered, and I need nothing, not realizing that you are wretched, pitiable, poor, blind, and naked" (Revelation 3:17). Such inflated spirits never get into the kingdom—and really do not care.

HANDLING WEALTH

Since wealth is so spiritually radioactive, the crucial question is how to handle it. And the answer begins by understanding that money doesn't belong to you. As seminary president Kenneth Kantzer once said:

We must give up all our wealth. We must own nothing. We are only stewards of what God owns. The point is not that we must be merely *willing* to give it up and then live like anyone else. Rather, we must actually give it up. We are to abandon completely any claims to the wealth of this world. It is not our own and we do not have ultimate control over it.[12]

Along with this understanding that our money is not our own, we must give it away joyfully. Theologian Jacques Ellul says that the only way to defeat the godlike power that money seeks to impose on our lives is to give it away, which he calls profaning it: "To profane money, like all other powers, is to take away its sacred character."[13] This destroys its power over us. "Giving to God is the act of profanation *par excellence*," says Ellul.[14] Every time I give, I declare that money does not control me. Perpetual generosity is a perpetual de-deification of money.

This makes great sense, and it cuts through the paralyzing controversies over affluence and individual lifestyle. Wherever you are on the economic continuum, you need to give generously and regularly. Generous giving as it relates to your affluence will free you from the bondage of money. You will be profaning money—declaring that it is not a god in your life. You can talk until the moon stands still about what is the proper lifestyle for a member of your church, and the result would be a corporate orgy of judgmentalism. And if we came up with a written description, it would entrench a grace-nullifying legalism. Paul minced no words with Timothy:

> *As for the rich in this present age, charge them not to be haughty, nor to set their hopes on the uncertainty of riches, but on God, who richly provides us with everything to enjoy. They are to do good, to be rich in good works, to be generous and ready to share, thus storing up treasure for themselves as a good foundation for the future, so that they may take hold of that which is truly life.*
>
> —1 TIMOTHY 6:17-19

This is the way to live—give, give, give!

In a similar vein, Paul told the Corinthians, "Each one must give as he has made up his mind, not reluctantly or under compulsion, for God loves a cheerful [hilarious] giver" (2 Corinthians 9:7). "The hilarity comes," says Yancey, ". . . because the art of giving is at its core irrational. It destroys the aura of worth surrounding money . . . giving flagrantly sets it free."[15] Giving doesn't make any sense to the materialist. It's crazy, "nuts." That's why it is so laughably joyous!

Personally I believe that our generosity ought to be to such an extent that it affects our lifestyles. Such giving means there are things and pleasures that we joyously forego, whether it be a new car or a coveted book or a golf club. And—should I mention it?—there is a divine windfall in all of this, and it is this: Money invested in the kingdom is the only money you'll ever see again! The promise comes straight from Jesus: "Do not lay up for yourselves treasures on earth, where moth and rust destroy and where thieves break in and steal, but lay up for yourselves treasures in heaven, where neither moth nor rust destroys and where thieves do not break in and steal. For where your treasure is, there your heart will be also" (Matthew 6:19-21).

Giving actually bears interest in heaven. I believe that. The divine "futures" will bear huge dividends. You'll see your money again.

I think that the graduated tithe is a great idea. The concept is simple: The giver begins with a basic tithe of 10 percent and then increases it yearly as God increases his annual provisions. The principle is that the more the giver prospers, the more he or she gives. To practice a graduated tithe requires that one prayerfully set goals to give 11 percent or 15 percent or 20 percent from one's earnings as God directs. I'm aware of a Greek professor in another city who gives 30 percent of his modest salary to his church and missions—and has done it five consecutive years.[16] Such commitments mean saying no to the ethos of consumerism. It means taking great care with your credit cards.

The important principle is this: *Those in the clutches of consumerism cannot practice stewardship.* To practice Christian stewardship means resisting the seductive voices of Victor Lebow's disciples, who tell us that we have to have everything *new* and *now*. It means cultivating the Christian virtues of contentment, self-denial, and generosity. The spiritual dividend is that untold resources will be freed for local ministry and world missions. Imagine what such giving would do for your church and the world!

The stakes are momentous. Our witness to the world is linked to setting ourselves apart from the world. As Christians, we have said yes to the things that are above—yes to being a coheir with Christ himself—yes to a place prepared for us—yes to riches stored up for us—yes to a crown—yes to co-regency with Christ! And in the light of this incredible yes, we must separate ourselves from the materialism of this world.

This is a matter of life and death. If the Gospel sets us free from the cancer of materialism, if we soar above the culture of materialism by the grace of Christ, then we will have good news to preach to lost, earthbound people.

FOR REFLECTION AND APPLICATION

- What are the symptoms of materialism in your life?
- In what ways does money exert its power over you?
- In what ways does materialism among Christians (either real or perceived) inhibit our witness to the Gospel?
- What steps can you take to "profane the god of money"?

NOTES

1. Jamie H. Thompson, "Am I Trying to Shock You?" at outreach.missouri.edu.
2. Rodney Clapp, "Why the Devil Takes Visa," *Christianity Today*, October 7, 1996, p. 27.
3. Ibid., pp. 27-28.
4. Barna Research Online, "The Year's Most Intriguing Findings." From Barna Research Studies, December 12, 2000.
5. Ibid.
6. Randy Alcorn, *Money, Possessions and Eternity* (Wheaton, IL: Tyndale, 1989), pp. 399-400.
7. David Neff, ed., *The Midas Trap* (Wheaton, IL: Victor, 1990), p. 21.
8. Alcorn, *Money, Possessions and Eternity*, p. 37.

9. Alan C. Emery, "Tools or Idols," in *A Turtle on a Fencepost* (Waco, TX: Word Books, 1979), pp. 33-37.

10. A. W. Tozer, "The Transmutation of Wealth," in *Born After Midnight* (Harrisburg, PA: Christian Publications, 1959), p. 107.

11. Philip Yancey, "Learning to Live with Money," *Christianity Today*, December 14, 1984, p. 35.

12. Neff, ed., *The Midas Trap*, p. 113.

13. Jacques Ellul, *Money & Power* (Downers Grove, IL: InterVarsity, 1984), p. 109.

14. Ibid., p. 111.

15. Yancey, "Learning to Live with Money," p. 40.

16. Craig L. Blomberg, *Neither Poverty nor Riches* (Downers Grove, IL: InterVarsity, 1999), p. 248 writes:

> When we were first married more than eighteen years ago, my wife and I committed to begin with a tithe, based on the very modest income we had while I was a graduate student, and then to increase that percentage if God increased his annual provisions for us. Over the years God has blessed us richly and the percentage of our giving has grown. On our last income-tax returns, we reported in the spring of 1998 our highest combined family income ever (a combination of my salary as a seminary professor, income from my wife's half-time church position and miscellaneous royalties, interests and dividends). Our overall total put us $4,000 below the average household income for our affluent suburban community. Nevertheless, we were able to give over 30% of our income to our church and to para-church organizations and individuals involved in Christian ministry. This was our fifth consecutive year of topping 30%, following the principle of the graduated tithe.

3

Set Apart to Save:
Hedonism

I said in my heart, "Come now, I will test you with pleasure; enjoy yourself." But behold, this also was vanity. I said of laughter, "It is mad," and of
pleasure, "What use is it?" I searched with my heart how to cheer my body
with wine—my heart still guiding me with wisdom—and how to lay hold
on folly, till I might see what was good for the children of man to do under
heaven during the few days of their life. I made great works. I built houses
and planted vineyards for myself. I made myself gardens and parks, and
planted in them all kinds of fruit trees. I made myself pools from which to
water the forest of growing trees. I bought male and female slaves, and had
slaves who were born in my house. I had also great possessions of herds
and flocks, more than any who had been before me in Jerusalem. I also
gathered for myself silver and gold and the treasure of kings and provinces.
I got singers, both men and women, and many concubines, the delight of
the children of man. So I became great and surpassed all who were before
me in Jerusalem. Also my wisdom remained with me. And whatever my
eyes desired I did not keep from them. I kept my heart from no pleasure,
for my heart found pleasure in all my toil, and this was my reward for all
my toil. Then I considered all that my hands had done and the toil I had
expended in doing it, and behold, all was vanity and a striving after wind,
and there was nothing to be gained under the sun.

ECCLESIASTES 2:1-11

Years ago two famous men produced opposite but equally chilling
visions for the twentieth century. George Orwell wrote *1984*, and
Aldous Huxley authored his *Brave New World*. Orwell warned that we
would be overcome by the external oppression of Big Brother. But
Huxley warned of an inner oppression in which people would love

the very things that oppressed them. In Orwell's *1984* people are controlled by inflicting pain. In Huxley's *Brave New World* they are controlled by inflicting pleasure.[1] Both models exist today in the cultures of the new millennium. But in the West, Huxley's vision is reality, as we are a culture controlled by pleasure.

Apart from the demands of work, the discretionary time of most Americans is controlled by the pursuit of pleasure. We are a culture of convenience. Calvin Miller has written, "Our love of convenience trains us to believe that we can have as much as we want, of whatever we want, whenever we want it. . . . No matter what life gives us, we always want more. . . . We are the walking wanton."[2]

Some spend whole days contemplating where and what the evening fare will be and what vintage will complement it, as though life itself depended on the choice. Many spend hours in inner debate over clothing labels because designer names are evocative of power and élan—even spiritual power. Lunch hours evaporate in discussions of what film or entertainment to see. Commuters escape into fantasies about Caribbean cruises prompted by advertisers who announce that you owe it to yourself because "the world revolves around you." Churchgoing retirees slip off for whole days to play the slots—"cheap entertainment," they say.[3] Hedonism has spawned a generation of thrill seekers and the phenomenon of extreme sports. Even worship is not exempt from hedonism as people go where worship is most pleasurable, imagining that the worship of God exists to make them feel good.

Today it is not Big Brother who controls us but Big Pleasure. And the oppression that the pursuit of pleasure exerts is far more controlling than fear because pleasure rules from the inside.

As with the sin of materialism, Christians must set themselves apart from the world's hedonistic pursuits if they are to have a ministry to the world. Lot, we remember, had balked at foregoing the pleasures of Sodom, with the sad result that he had little or no impact on Sodom's dying culture. In contrast Moses rejected "the fleeting pleasures of sin" in Egypt with the result that he was used to effect the deliverance of his people (cf. Hebrews 11:25).

If we are captive to the pursuit of pleasure, there is little chance that we will introduce others to the pleasures of God. Our singular hope, and by extension the hope for those we would attempt to influence for Christ, is to let the Scriptures define and direct our pleasures.

PLEASURE IN SCRIPTURE

Enjoy pleasure! What God's Word actually says may surprise some because it declares earthly pleasures good and invites God's people to enjoy them! Everything in God's creation is good. Six times during the act of creation God declared it to be "good," with the final pronouncement emphatically stating creation to be "very good" (Genesis 1:31). The apostle Paul reaffirmed this to Timothy to steel him against an ascetic rejection of the world, saying, "For everything created by God is good, and nothing is to be rejected if it is received with thanksgiving" (1 Timothy 4:4). The Bible never treats physical and earthly pleasures as intrinsically bad, in deference to spiritual pleasures as the only good or legitimate pleasures. Asceticism (the denial of physical pleasures) has thrived on the false assumption that physical pleasures are evil. This is simply not so.

Leland Ryken, editor of *Dictionary of Biblical Imagery*, categorically demonstrates in his entry on "Pleasures" that earthly pleasures are divinely ordained. Ryken lists six God-given categories of human pleasure.[4] They are:

• *Nature* is a divinely given source of pleasure and is celebrated by five nature poems in the Psalms that sing of the stars and rain and grass and seasons with soul-stirring imagery and passion (cf. Psalms 8, 19, 29, 104, 148).

• *Human artistry*. The Scriptures also commend our taking pleasure in human artistry, such as the exquisite craftsmanship in the tabernacle and in the temple (cf. Exodus 31:1-11; 1 Kings 7:15-22) and the sound of a harp (Psalm 81:2) and the writing of "words of delight" (Ecclesiastes 12:10).

• *Family* is commended by God as a great repository of pleasure. The parent whose quiver is full of children is "blessed [happy]"

(Psalm 127:5). Grandchildren are exalted as a source of pleasure (Psalm 128:6).

• *Romantic love and sexual fulfillment.* Proverbs 5:18-19 is a brief celebration of the sexual pleasures of married life. The Song of Songs elaborates on the joys of romantic passion.

• *Social life and community* are likewise God-ordained vehicles of pleasure. Pilgrimages and divinely appointed festivals enhance the pleasures of like-minded people dwelling together in joyous community (cf. Psalm 133). Jesus himself contributed to the joy of family celebrations (cf. John 2).

• *Corporate worship.* And, of course, corporate worship is a prominent source of pleasure—"I was glad when they said to me, 'Let us go to the house of the LORD!'" (Psalm 122:1; cf. Psalm 84).

God-given pleasure is everywhere in life. A main theme of the Bible is that we don't have to look far for pleasure. It's everywhere around us. According to Scripture, virtually any aspect of daily life is innately pleasurable. Land (Psalm 106:24), speech (Proverbs 16:21, 24), riches (Proverbs 24:4), and sleep (Psalm 4:8; 127:2) are all sources of pleasure. The mere light of the sun makes the writer of Ecclesiastes rapturous (11:7).

The enjoyment of these human pleasures is independent of wealth and status, as the following luminous testimony from an anonymous eighteenth-century woman ("A Poor Methodist Woman" was her pen name) so eloquently expresses:

> I do not know when I have had happier times in my soul than when I have been sitting at work, with nothing before me but a candle and a white cloth, and hearing no sound but that of my own breath; with God in my soul and heaven in my eye. I rejoice in being exactly what I am—a creature capable of loving God, and who, as long as God lives, must be happy. I get up and look a while out the window. I gaze at the moon and stars, the work of an Almighty Hand. I think of the grandeur of the universe and then sit down and think myself one of the happiest beings in it.

Pleasures everywhere. My own experience testifies to the fact that God's good creation places his pleasure at every turn. Like you, I've had dramatic experiences of his earthly pleasures at times. Years ago when we lived in California, I went fishing off Cabo San Lucas, and late in the afternoon we dropped anchor in an emerald bay, donned snorkels, and slipped over the side into beauty then unparalleled in our experience—shimmering forms, yellows and aquamarines, slowly waving grass—the pleasurable hidden creation of God. And again that night, when we lifted up our eyes from the phosphorous streaks of fish fleeing before the boat's bow and gazed at the spring constellations, it was with intense pleasure. The same thing sometimes happens to us on winter nights in Wisconsin.

Then there are the intense pleasures of human artistry. For me, certain artists like William Blake, Samuel Palmer, and lately especially Matisse have given me intense pleasure. There is also always the pleasure of words. And there are the recurrent pleasures of beloved musical pieces—a hymn, an aria, a child's melody. Of course family is a primary source of pleasure. Few earthly pleasures can surpass the beloved geography of family faces around the table, all singing the Doxology. And I have to say there are also the pleasures of a good meal. It's wonderful to be married to a great cook who has spoiled me with her herbal artistry. Certainly there will be fresh basil in heaven and acres of cilantro! And worship—what pleasure there is in joining with the corporate voices of brothers and sisters in praise and prayer to God.

The pleasures are everywhere indeed. And I think common pleasures can be more acute for believers because they are at peace with the Creator of all pleasures—every good thing. God is a "hedonist" whose pleasure is to pour delights on all creation. In fact, John Piper has written two whole books on the theme of God's pleasure in being God and in bestowing pleasures on his creatures (the books are provocatively entitled *Desiring God: Confessions of a Christian Hedonist* and *The Pleasures of God: Meditation on God's Delight in Being God*).

God's pleasures need no pursuit, because they are at hand. It is our duty to enjoy them.

Pursue pleasure? To pursue pleasures as an end in themselves is folly. Solomon reflects on his experience in chapters 1—2 of Ecclesiastes, where he reveals that he thought in his heart, "Come now, I will test you with pleasure; enjoy yourself" (2:1). So Solomon proceeded to explore a vast range of pleasures—a path that many others have attempted, and with parallel results. In fact, Solomon pursued pleasure in the very places where our culture pursues it, as this single brief narrative chronicles virtually the entire gamut where our contemporary culture chases after pleasure.

Initially Solomon pursued happiness in *mental endeavors* (the pursuit of knowledge).

> *I said in my heart, "I have acquired great wisdom, surpassing all who were over Jerusalem before me, and my heart has had great experience of wisdom and knowledge." And I applied my heart to know wisdom and to know madness and folly. I perceived that this also is but a striving after wind. For in much wisdom is much vexation, and he who increases knowledge increases sorrow.*
>
> —1:16-18

Next, he turned to *laughter* (the escape into comedy) for satisfaction. But it failed him. "I said of laughter, 'It is mad,' and of pleasure, 'What use is it?'" (2:2). Then Solomon sought pleasure in *wine*: "I searched with my heart how to cheer my body with wine—my heart still guiding me with wisdom—and how to lay hold on folly, till I might see what was good for the children of man to do under heaven during the few days of their life" (v. 3). Predictably he found no satisfaction. As he said in the Proverbs, "Wine is a mocker, strong drink a brawler, and whoever is led astray by it is not wise" (20:1).

Turning from the abyss of drink, he embarked on *grand projects* (the acquisitive spirit): "I made great works. I built houses and planted vineyards for myself. I made myself gardens and parks, and planted in them all kinds of fruit trees. I made myself pools from which to water the forest of growing trees" (2:4-6). But the rush of building pleasures subsided when the projects were completed.

Next Solomon concentrated on amassing *wealth*: "I bought male and female slaves, and had slaves who were born in my house. I had also great possessions of herds and flocks, more than any who had been before me in Jerusalem. I also gathered for myself silver and gold and the treasure of kings and provinces" (vv. 7-8a.). But this did not bring happiness. Three chapters later he gives this aphorism: "He who loves money will not be satisfied with money, nor he who loves wealth with his income; this also is vanity" (5:10).

Along with his riches, the king pursued the escape of *sex*: "I got singers, both men and women, and many concubines, the delight of the children of man" (2:8b.). However a thousand wives and concubines did not satisfy Solomon. In truth, his sexual excesses led him astray (cf. 1 Kings 11:3-4). The reference to singers, incidentally, hints at yet another modern-looking quest—the pursuit of entertainment.

Solomon achieved worldly *fame*: "So I became great and surpassed all who were before me in Jerusalem. Also my wisdom remained with me" (v. 9). The Queen of Sheba heard of Solomon's fame, and when see saw it she declared, "And behold, the half was not told me" (1 Kings 10:7).[5]

Solomon had tested himself with pleasure and had done it all, pursuing, as he describes it, *wisdom* and *laughter* and *wine* and *great works* and *riches* and *sex* and *fame*—every pleasure. And what did he learn? Solomon states it in these memorable words:

> *And whatever my eyes desired I did not keep from them. I kept my heart from no pleasure, for my heart found pleasure in all my toil, and this was my reward for all my toil. Then I considered all that my hands had done and the toil I had expended in doing it, and behold, all was vanity and a striving after wind, and there was nothing to be gained under the sun.*
> —ECCLESIASTES 2:10-11

So it has been with every man and woman who has pursued pleasure as an end in itself. This is the autobiography and obituary of every hedonist who has ever lived. Do not be deceived by the self-assured rhetoric of the Donald Trumps of this world or the fawning hedonistic delusion of *People* magazine. For such lives, "all is vanity and a striving after wind, and there is nothing to be gained under the sun."

THE PERVERSION OF PLEASURES

As we have said, God's creation and the earthly pleasures he spreads around us are good. The problem with pleasure is not pleasure itself, but what we and the Devil do with it. There is a brilliantly instructive passage in C. S. Lewis's *Screwtape Letters* where he has the senior devil say to his understudy Wormwood:

> Never forget that when we are dealing with any pleasure in its healthy and normal and satisfying form, we are, in a sense, on the Enemy's ground. I know we have won many a soul through pleasure. All the same, it is His invention, not ours. He made the pleasures: all our research so far has not enabled us to produce one. All we can do is to encourage the humans to take the pleasures which our Enemy has produced, at times, or in ways, or in degrees, which He has forbidden. Hence we always try to work away from the natural condition of any pleasure to that in which it is least natural, least redolent of its Maker, and least pleasurable. An ever increasing craving for an ever diminishing pleasure is the formula.[6]

Much later in the book, Lewis has Screwtape declare, "He has filled His world full of pleasures. There are things for humans to do all day long without His minding in the least—sleeping, washing, eating, drinking, making love, playing, praying, working. Everything has to be *twisted* before it's any use to us."[7]

When and how, then, does pleasure become twisted? First, when we forget that all pleasure is a gift from God and imagine that it is something that we can have apart from him. Fullness of pleasure cannot be had apart from the Ultimate Hedonist, the creator and bestower of eternal pleasures.

Second, pleasure becomes twisted when it becomes a pursuit instead of something that we accept with gratitude from the hand of God. There are lavish pleasures at every hand in creation, art, family, love, sex, food, community, and worship. Those who chase headlong after evanescent pleasures run right by the best things—and end up striving after the wind. We don't have to pursue pleasures, only *receive* them. As Ray Stedman asks:

> Isn't it strange that the more you run after life, panting after every pleasure, the less you find, but the more you take life as a gift from God's hand, responding in thankful gratitude for the delight of the moment, the more that seems to come to you? Even the trials, the heartaches and handicaps that others seek to avoid are touched with the blessing of heaven and seem to minister to the heart of the one who has learned to take them from the hand of God.[8]

In a similar vein, Derek Kidner comments on "the paradox of hedonism": "the more you hunt for pleasure, the less of it you find."[9]

Third, pleasure becomes perverted when we consider it our right, or in today's language an entitlement that merits instant gratification. Such attitudes grab at pleasures, only to discover that all they possess is air.

Fourth, all God's earthly pleasures become grotesquely twisted when they are overindulged. A memorable meal with friends is a gift from God. But when we decide that every meal must be memorable—when our stomach becomes our god—we become idolaters, indulging "an ever increasing craving for an ever diminishing pleasure." Nature's beauty is a universal gift. But for some the outdoors becomes an end in itself, and God who thought it and spoke it into existence becomes a forgotten footnote in a desolate life.

THE HARM OF HEDONISM

The harm of hedonism is a matter of empirical record. When pleasure-seeking characterizes a person's life, it invariably means an inversion of priorities. Giving pleasure first place demeans and reorders every other priority. The enthronement of a pleasurable pursuit, be it a hobby like fishing or antiquing, or an intellectual pleasure or an aesthetic pursuit, puts everything else in life in second and third and fourth place—your spouse, your children, your parents, your friends, your church. You may now be the best tennis player in Chicago or the best quilter or the best bass fisherman in the county or the most knowledgeable history buff in five states. And when you die that's what you'll be—and little else. "Wow! What a great largemouth fisherman Dad was!" "Mom looks peaceful buried in her quilt. Wish I had known her."

And there's more. The inversion of priorities diminishes the enjoyment of the good pleasures of God that are so freely strewn around us. An obsessive pursuit of pleasure leaves no time for the pleasures of creation and family and feasting and conversation and the worship of God.

The pathology goes deeper. Pleasure-seeking is by definition an avoidance of pain. But pain and suffering are essential to the Christian for growth, maturity, and usefulness. No pain, no gain. Hedonism shrinks the self to a tiny self-focus that diminishes your usability not only to God, but to those you love most. Pleasure-seeking instills a retreat from ministry. Pleasure-seekers have nothing to say to the world. Pleasure-seekers don't care.

Lastly, pleasure-seeking anesthetizes the seeker to his or her need. The intermittent rushes of pleasure that come from their pursuits dull pleasure-seekers to their own spiritual need. The inordinate pursuit of pleasures, be they stock car races, the city's best eateries, shopping, golf, gardening, film, astronomy—*all good things in themselves*—can supply enough distraction to keep you from reflecting on what is really important.

THE GRAND HEDONISM

Aldous Huxley had it right. Today's culture is controlled by inflicting pleasure, and we are part of that culture. But as believers we must learn to say no to those pleasures that would draw us away from God, our family, our church, and those in need. We, not our material possessions, nor the media, nor the promise of pleasure, must take control of our lives!

Are you pursuing pleasures that are diminishing the deep pleasures that God has placed at your fingertips? Are the pleasures of cars and boats, of dining, of entertainments, of sports, of hobbies, of legal sensualities taking control of your life? Take control back.

The key to all of this is the grand hedonism of the Bible. Our greatest pleasure resides in God, and will always be in him. The classic text for the Christian hedonist is Psalm 16, with its famous pleasure images, culminating with the final lines:

> *You make known to me the path of life;*
> *in your presence there is fullness of joy;*
> *at your right hand are pleasures forevermore.*

> —V. 11

> There is pleasure and more pleasure. He makes no secret of it; at his right hand are 'pleasures for evermore' . . . He has filled the world full of pleasures.[10]

God wants us to be happy—in him. God wants us to immerse ourselves in his pleasure by immersing ourselves in him. John Piper put it this way, making a slight alteration of the opening line of the Westminster Confession:

> *The chief end of man is to glorify God*
> *BY*
> *enjoying Him forever.*[11]

God's desire to be glorified and your desire to be satisfied are one! Pursue him with all you have. It is this eternal, God-centered pleasure that will give you the power to say no to the deadly pursuit of pleasure. God calls us to moderation. He calls us sometimes to embrace pain. He calls us to *receive* pleasures rather than to seek them. He calls us to forego some pleasures for his sake, and the sake of our families, and the sake of the church—and the world.

We must set ourselves apart from hedonism so that we might have a message for our pleasure-mad world.

FOR REFLECTION AND APPLICATION

• What are the symptoms of inappropriate pleasure-seeking in your life?

• In what ways does your pursuit of pleasure involve an "inversion of priorities," displacing higher pursuits such as worship, ministry, fellowship, and service?

• Are there pleasures in which you overindulge? How can you control this?

• What steps should you take to pursue finding your true pleasure in God?

NOTES

1. Neil Postman, *Amusing Ourselves to Death* (New York: Viking, 1989), p. viii.
2. Calvin Miller, *The Unchained Soul* (Minneapolis: Bethany House, 1998).
3. John W. Kennedy, "Gambling Away the Golden Years," *Christianity Today*, May 24, 1999, Vol. 43, No. 6, p. 40.
4. Leland Ryken, James C. Wilhoit, and Tremper Longman III, general editors, *Dictionary of Biblical Imagery* (Downers Grove, IL: InterVarsity Press, 1998), pp. 651-654.
5. Norman Geisler, "The Christian As Pleasure Seeker," *Christianity Today*, September 26, 1975, pp. 11-12. Note: I have closely reproduced Geisler's brief exposition. The order and the insights are his, though I have altered the language for the most part.
6. C. S. Lewis, *Screwtape Letters and Screwtape Proposes a Toast* (London: Geoffrey Books, 1961), p. 50.

7. Ibid., p. 100.

8. Ray Stedman, *Is This All There Is to Life?* (Palo Alto, CA: Discovery House, 1999), pp. 651-654.

9. Derek Kidner, *A Time to Mourn, and a Time to Dance* (Leicester, England: Inter-Varsity, 1976), p. 51.

10. Lewis, *Screwtape Letters and Screwtape Proposes a Toast*, p. 100.

11. John Piper, *Desiring God* (Portland: Multnomah, 1986), p. 14.

4

Set Apart to Save:
Viewing Sensuality

Finally, brothers, whatever is true, whatever is honorable, whatever is just, whatever is pure, whatever is lovely, whatever is commendable, if there is any excellence, if there is anything worthy of praise, think about these things.

PHILIPPIANS 4:8

In 1932, when Aldous Huxley envisioned a *Brave New World* controlled by inflicting pleasure, he could not have imagined the thoroughgoing power of television as the instrument of pleasure's tyranny. Today the all-pervasive glow of the television set is the single most potent influence and control in western culture. Television has greater power over the lives of most Americans than any educational system or government or church. It is the control center of most homes—more ubiquitous and more controlling than Orwell's Big Brother.

And nowhere is television flexing its muscle more than in the alteration of America's sexual mores and practices. In a 1997 report before the Senate Subcommittee on Oversight of Government Management, anthropologist Dr. David Murray argued persuasively that "TV proselytizes sexuality," that the young of our culture are being socialized in their sexual behavior by the examples and values of television. Dr. Murray first demonstrated that there is a massive disconnect between sexual practices in the actual world and the world of television. He pointed out that the 1994 University of Chicago and National Research Center study "The Social Organization of Sexuality" found that the real, everyday world is one of sexual restraint. This study, based on a survey of 3,500 adults, indicated that a casual pickup with a stranger is rare—especially exotic strangers. A Kaiser Foundation report on the same group indicates that 90 percent of wives and 75 percent of husbands are faithfully monogamous. And more, only 5.8 percent of all couples were living together outside of marriage. Homosexuality constitutes 1 to 2 percent of women and between 3 and 5 percent of men, depending on how the category is defined. Overall the Chicago sociologists say that this culture is "not as obsessed with sex in [their] private lives as [they] are in popular culture."[1]

In stark contrast to the everyday world is the culture of contemporary American prime-time television—the culture of "Hypersex." Says Dr. Murray:

> Television presents sexuality in a manner that is not only pervasive, it is treated as an exotic imperative, ungovernable, lusty, smoldering, involving impossibly perfect sexual athletes who are nearly Olympian in their beauty and bodily enhancement. Further, it offers their behavior as normative, natural, expected, condoned, and even to be encouraged.[2]

Thus we have two Americas: the eroticized of television and the normal as life is lived. And, as you would fear, the situation is not static because prime-time television is socializing our young with its values and behavior. The boundary between the real world and the virtual world is becoming increasingly unclear.

Empirical data shows that television has become increasingly sexual in the last three decades. A media content analysis conducted by the Center for Media and Public Affairs shows that prior to 1969 fewer than one instance of extramarital sex occurred in every thirty shows. During the 1970s, extramarital sex was featured in one out of eight shows. Since the mid-1970s, the ratio has become one in six shows and is becoming more frequent. In 1987 a year-long study conducted by the Planned Parenthood Federation calculated that no fewer than sixty-five thousand references to sex were broadcast on television during the prime afternoon and evening hours. This gives an *hourly average* of ten sexual innuendoes and between one and two references to intercourse and "deviant or discouraged sexual practices." Bottom line: The average American TV viewer (who watches about four hours plus per day) sees some fourteen thousand instances of sexual material per year![3]

The last decade of the twentieth century witnessed a drastic increase in sensual viewing, with the per hour statistics tripling. Tellingly, references to homosexuality were rare in 1989, but in 1999 they had become mainstream—twenty-four times more common.[4] Along with this tripling of sexual material, married sexuality is actually played down. In the spring of 1991, researchers for the American Family Association noted that sexual activity in prime time favored sex outside marriage thirteen to one.[5] Terry Fisher, one of the producers of *L.A. Law*, said with revealing candor, "For television, married or celibate characters aren't as much fun."[6]

TV's agenda. There is a revealing connection between the increase of salacious TV and the background of TV executives as compared with the viewing public. Only 7 percent of those executives attend church regularly, as compared with 55 percent of the viewing public; 44 percent have no religious affiliation, whereas only 10 percent of viewers have no such affiliation.[7] To deny that there is a conscious assault on Christian values and sexual mores is like believing that Al Qaeda is building a "kinder, gentler world."

As Dr. Murray pointed out to the Senate subcommittee, prime-time programming is dictated first by profit and second by a moral agenda dictated by the elites who control the media. Entertainment has become "advotainment" that attempts to guide Americans toward trends dissonant with their values. As one discerning critic said, "There are fewer oxymorons as delightful as a Hollywood producer on a moral crusade."[8]

TV's effects. The negative effects of television are notorious.

First, *television promotes passivity.* Television watching is innately passive. The viewer listlessly watches images on the screen. Real life becomes too requiring. The viewer can imagine he's "done it" by virtue of simply watching it!

Television shortens attention span. Today many people find it difficult to focus on reasoned speech apart from visual images. Fleeting images do not produce thought—only reactions. When people are thus conditioned, they find it hard to concentrate.

Television inhibits thinking. A *Garfield* cartoon pictures Garfield watching TV with his eyelids half-closed. His friend asks, "What are you watching, Garfield?" "I don't know." "Who's the lead character?" "I don't know." "What's the plot?" "Hey! I'm watching television! Stop making me think, okay?"

In truth, when moving images dominate the written or spoken word, reason subsides. Thinking requires a certain distance and time to reflect, whereas moving images demand involvement and voyeurism—not thought.[9]

Television creates distance. As Ann Landers put it, "Television has proved that people will look at anything rather than each other."[10] I once spent an evening in a home where the host sat in a Lazyboy, his face luminous in the tube's nether-light. He never turned his head from the screen for conversation—which was really only a detached series of comments rather than a dialogue. Only when we left did he make eye contact. And as we walked out the driveway I saw he was back in his Lazyboy facing a flickering screen.

These effects are bad enough, but more pernicious things assault the average four-hour-per-day viewer. As we have said, our sexuality is proselytized and eroticized by the TV world with scripts and templates for future action. Millions of Christians have been desensitized and sensualized as they sit passively night after night in prime time before lewdness and double entendre without the slightest twinge of conscience.

Along with this, *TV watching inculcates irreverence for God.* Film critic Michael Medved, writing in 1990, said that the record for expletives goes to the Martin Scorsese film *GoodFellas*, which had 272 expletives, 246 of which were variations of one single word. There was a major obscenity every 32.2 seconds![11] Of course, this has been eclipsed today in gangster rap movies. Interestingly, no one seems to be counting the blasphemous abuse of God's name—the number of times "God" and "O God!" are used as fillers for absent syntax, and "Jesus" and "Christ" as angry exclamation points. In the movies men employ the name "God" in such a way as to effect swagger and a "devil may care" élan. And female stars regularly use God's name with fashionable intonation to communicate a worldly-wise, urbanely-bored air.

God is debased on every side and in ways so subtle that Christians do not even take notice. But their inner computers do—as a spirit of blasphemy infuses their souls. Sometimes God's holy name becomes the compulsive rhetorical filler in a Christian's ever-emptying life. But we must not forget God's Word: "You shall not take the name of the LORD your God in vain, for the LORD will not hold him guiltless who takes his name in vain" (Exodus 20:7).

Perhaps the most subtle of television's evils is *the promotion of worldviews that are sub-Christian and spiritually destructive.* Disney is no protection. *The Little Mermaid* is innocent enough if you ignore the storyline, which says, follow your heart, ignore your parents. Any junior-high girl who watched *Titanic* multiple times (some watched thirteen or fourteen times, as the papers reported) has drunk deeply of a worldview that is minus God, that is sensually hedonistic, that is superficial and sentimental to the nth degree. She has learned that a one-night affair may be expected to be the apex of her life; that instant sex will buy her sacrificial love; that the ultimate in life is to pursue your own pleasures (in the protagonist's life she pursues her own pleasures into old age), and that the glory of old age comes from the sins of her youth.

Some of you (and I hope it is many) are not in the thrall of television. But the statistics reveal that the viewing habits of Christians are generally the *same* as the rest of culture. This means that between the age of six and eighteen the average child will watch fifteen thousand to sixteen thousand hours of TV.[12] And during the first twenty years of a child's life, he or she will see some one million commercials at the rate of one thousand per week![13]

The television is on seven hours and fifteen minutes daily in the average home, and the average person watches it over four hours each day or about thirty hours per week. A study of three thousand children by the Kaiser Foundation reveals that 53 percent of all children between the ages of two and eighteen have a TV set in their own bedroom. And 49 percent say that their parents exert no controls.[14] Ah, family togetherness! "Mom and Dad have a TV in their bedroom, junior is watching in the den, sissy has her own set in her bedroom."[15]

But are the viewing habits of Christian *adults* really identical to the rest of culture? Sadly, yes. The April 2000 study by the Pew Research Center for The People and The Press Biennial Media Consumption Survey reveals very little difference.

Percentage who said they *"regularly watch the following . . .*	*General* *Population*	*Born Again* *Christian*★
How often do you watch		
CBS, ABC, or NBC?	30	31
How often do you watch		
CNN?	21	22
CNBC	13	12
FoxNews	18	21
R. Lake or J. Springer	7	10

★ Responded "yes" to the question "Would you describe yourself as a 'born again' or evangelical Christian, or not?"[16]

Many of us are exceptions. But the statistics are alarming for the evangelical church. There is no way around it: The church must be set apart in its viewing habits if it is to remain healthy. The daily viewing of sensuality, double entendre, and base humor makes it impossible for the viewer to effectively maintain a clean heart. Those who visit *Christianity Today's* website are asked to indicate their favorite TV program, and the overwhelmingly preferred choice of younger viewers is *Friends*, which portrays the everyday lives of a group of singles preoccupied with sex and witty double entendre. The show is wickedly funny, wherein lies the depth of its evil. As Malcolm Muggeridge, British writer, TV host, and editor of the legendary humor magazine *Punch*, pointed out, when we are enticed to laugh about immorality, our resistance is weakened. And if we laugh enough, we become susceptible to those sins.[17] Tragically, a sensualized church has little or nothing to say to a world in sensual bondage. It is of utmost importance that we set ourselves apart from sensual input if we wish to have a witness to this lost world. Our very distinctiveness as Christ's children is at the base of any witness we may wish to have.

WHAT THE BIBLE SAYS

When we turn to God's Word, we are aware that the biblical writers understood the problem in a less technical, though more personally beneficial way. "Keep your heart with all vigilance," says Proverbs, "for from it flow the springs of life" (Proverbs 4:23). "For as he thinks within himself, so he is" (Proverbs 23:7, NASB). The Scriptures tell us rightly that input determines output—that our programming determines production.

In the New Testament, no one understood this better than the apostle Paul. In fact, in his letter to the Philippians, after alluding to guarding the heart, Paul prescribed his personal program in one sublime sentence: "Finally, brothers, whatever is true, whatever is honorable, whatever is just, whatever is pure, whatever is lovely, whatever is commendable, if there is any excellence, if there is anything worthy of praise, think about these things" (Philippians 4:8). Each of Paul's ingredients is explicitly positive. The true, the honorable, the just, the pure, the lovely, and the commendable all defy negative exposition. Each ingredient was, and is, *a matter of personal choice*—and our choices make all the difference in the world.

Paul's challenge to "*think* about these things" is a loaded charge. The word he uses is *logidzomai*, from which we get the mathematical, computer-like word *logarithm*. It means a "deliberate and prolonged contemplation, as if one is weighing a mathematical problem."[18] The way I handle my mail gives an example. Frankly, most of it gets tossed. I read the return address to see if it is an ad, perhaps open it, scan a few lines—and away it goes. But if it is an outdoor catalog, it gets deliberate and prolonged contemplation. We are to think about the wonderful elements God wants us to put into our mental and spiritual computers.

At the same time, as we consider how Paul's program should affect our minds, the sheer weight of its positives demands a determined rejection of negative input: "Finally, brothers, whatever is untrue, whatever is dishonorable, whatever is unjust, whatever is impure, whatever is unlovely, whatever is unadmirable—if there is anything shoddy or unworthy of praise—do not think about these things." It was not that Paul was naive. He knew the dark side of human experience. Romans 1 proves that. But he chose not to make such input a part of his mental programming.

In some cases this may call for extreme action: "If your right eye causes you to sin, tear it out and throw it away," says Jesus (Matthew 5:29). The Psalmist likewise gave sage advice for those living in the media age: "I will walk with integrity of heart within my house; I will not set before my eyes anything that is worthless" (Psalm 101:2b-3a). We must allow Christ to be Lord of our prime time.

WHAT TO DO

TV, a spiritual matter. We must first understand that our use of the television is a spiritual matter. In respect to sensuality and sexual sins, we must understand that God detests immorality among his people— and that we ought to feel aversion and anger at the grip of sensuality on our culture.

We ought to be mirrors of God's character to our culture. Prime-time sensuality offends God and ought to offend us. God's Word says, "O you who love the LORD, hate evil!" (Psalm 97:10). God, through Jeremiah, condemns those who do not know how to blush (Jeremiah 8:12). Paul declares that "it is shameful even to speak of the things that they do in secret" (Ephesians 5:12).

Philosopher and theologian Mark R. Talbot, writing on the subject of "Godly Emotions," explains, "Strong negative emotions are important indicators of who—and *whose*—we are. To claim to be Christian and yet not to feel emotional aversion when Christian moral standards are violated is, at best, to exhibit a kind of mental schizophrenia between our heads and hearts."[19] To feel no emotion about this means that we are captive to culture—that the media has got us—that we are worldly. Get angry in the Lord! But do not sin (cf. Ephesians 4:26).

Next, if you are married, get together with your spouse, bare your heart, and pray about what you ought to do. Don't be impulsive. Don't do something that you will later regret. Don't overreact. Let God's Word, the counsel of your spouse, and prayer guide you. Then act.

Take control of your TV. Determine that you are not going to passively allow television to control your souls. This involves a determination to limit the time you watch it, select what you watch, and turn it off when it *begins* to offend, not *after* it offends. In order to gain control of the medium, you may want to take a month's fast from the tube. Bob DeMoss's *TV The Great Escape, Life-Changing Stories from Those Who Dared to Take Control* records the feedback of more than fifty families who agreed to turn off their TV's for a month. He doesn't call for a permanent boycott but invites you to find a balance that enriches your life. If you can't control it, throw it out! If the eye of your cathode tube offends you, tear it out. Better to go through life with no TV than into hell with your remote in hand.

Control your children's TV. In light of the immense challenge that the media represent to our families, we must remember that Deuteronomy 6 lays out the primary duty of parents to instruct their children in the teachings of God's Word: "You shall teach them diligently to your children, and shall talk of them when you sit in your house, and when you walk by the way, and when you lie down, and when you rise" (Deuteronomy 6:7). This cannot be done with the TV on. It requires careful parental control and discipline.

Among the essentials is to painstakingly limit your children's TV watching. One couple in my church sits down weekly with their children with the *TV Guide* and allots them two hours of watching. The children choose with their parents' approval what they will watch. This has worked well. It's also essential to watch some of your children's programs with them, offering some perspective if necessary. Never allow television sets in your children's bedrooms. This is also good advice for the dining room as well as Mom and Dad's bedroom. Keep TVs (and computers) where everyone can see what's on. Conduct an inventory of the videos in your home, and toss out those that are offensive. If you're going to rent a video, check it out on the websites that do movie reviews. For more information on trustworthy movie reviews online (as well as Internet filters and Internet safety tips), see Appendix II.

CONCLUSION

We are called to be holy. If we define holiness merely as being separated from sin, we miss the whole thing. A careful reading of the book of Leviticus reveals that holiness does much more than separate us from uncleanness. It is freedom from uncleanness, but it is also harmony with God. What great benefits accrue from holiness! If we set ourselves apart, we have *harmony* with God and *freedom* from unclean things. And then we will have great power in sharing the Gospel with a lost culture under the domination of wicked people with wicked intent. We must take control. We have to do it. Let's do it!

FOR REFLECTION AND APPLICATION

- How has television benefited your spiritual life?
- How has television detracted from your spiritual life? Be specific.
- What examples of a sensual worldview can you think of?
- How can you cultivate moral aversion and even anger toward pervasive sensuality?
- What changes can you make to "think about such things" as listed in Philippians 4:8?

NOTES

1. www.stats.org/record.jsp?type=news&id=408, Testimony of David Murray, Ph.D., before Senate Subcommittee on Oversight of Government Management, Restructuring, and the District of Columbia, of the Committee on Governmental Affairs, May 8, 1997, p. 2.

2. Ibid., p. 3.

3. Ibid., p. 4.

4. www.probe.org/does/sex-viol.html, Kerby Anderson, *Sex and Violence on Television*, p. 1, which quotes from Parents Television Council, *Special Report: What a Difference a Decade Makes*, March 30, 2000, p. 1, www.parentstv.org.

5. Michael Medved, *Hollywood vs. America* (New York: Harper Collins, 1992), p. 112.

   In the "Spring Sweeps" period of 1991 (April 28-May 25), researchers for the American Family Association logged a total of 615 instances of sexual activity depicted or discussed on prime-time shows. By a margin of *thirteen to one* (571 to 44) these references favored sex outside of marriage over intimate relations between life partners.

6. Ibid., p. 111.

7. George Barna and William Paul McKay, *Vital Signs* (Wheaton, IL: Crossway Books, 1984), p. 56, who reference Linda Lichter, S. Robert Lichter, and Stanley Rothman, "Hollywood and America: The Odd Couple," *Public Opinion*, January 1983, pp. 54-58.

8. Murray, p. 6.

9. Douglas S. Groothuis, "How the Bombarding Images of TV Culture Undermine the Power of Words," *Modern Reformation*, January/February 2001, p. 33.

10. Bob DeMoss, Jr., *TV The Great Escape* (Wheaton, IL: Crossway Books, 2001), p. 41.

11. Medved, *Hollywood vs. America*, p. 179.

12. Neil Postman, "TV's 'Disastrous' Impact on Children," *U.S. News and World Report*, January 19, 1981, p. 43.

13. Ibid., p. 44.

14. DeMoss, *TV The Great Escape,* p. 27.

15. Ibid., p. 33.

16. April 2000 Biennial Media Consumption Survey by the Pew Research Center for The People and The Press.

17. Malcolm Muggeridge, *Christ and the Media* (Grand Rapids, MI: Eerdmans, 1977).

18. A. T. Robertson, *Paul's Joy in Christ* (Grand Rapids, MI: Baker, 1979), p. 242.

19. Mark R. Talbot, "Godly Emotions," *Modern Reformation*, Vol. 10, No. 6, November/December 2002, pp. 32-37. This particular quotation is found on the Alliance of Confessing Evangelicals website at www.alliancenet.org.

5

Set Apart to Save:
Violence and Voyeurism

Lamech said to his wives: "Adah and Zillah, hear my voice; you wives of Lamech, listen to what I say: I have killed a man for wounding me, a young man for striking me." . . . Now the earth was corrupt in God's sight, and the earth was filled with violence. And God saw the earth, and behold, it was corrupt, for all flesh had corrupted their way on the earth. And God said to Noah, "I have determined to make an end of all flesh. . . . For behold, I will bring a flood of waters upon the earth to destroy all flesh in which is the breath of life under heaven. Everything that is on the earth shall die."

GENESIS 4:23; 6:11-13, 17

If Lamech's song were sung today, I would imagine a shirtless, well-muscled man with barbed-wire bandoliers tattooed across his bare chest, gripping his assault rifle as he intones his vengeance rap style:

"Adah and Zillah, hear my voice;
you wives of Lamech, listen to what I say:
I have killed a man for wounding me, a young man for striking me.
If Cain's revenge is sevenfold, then Lamech's is seventy-sevenfold."
—GENESIS 4:23-24

Lamech boasted of his merciless heart. He had killed a young man (Hebrew *yeled*, "child") for a mere wound. Lamech wore violence as a badge of honor and gloried in exponential vengeance. Lamech's soul indulged in a demonic ecstasy. So dark. So ugly. His was the song of the godless descendants of Cain—of the Cainite civilization. Cainite depravity was then countered by Seth's godly line and a people who began "to call on the name of the LORD" (4:26) and who produced the great man Enoch, who "walked with God, and he was not, for God took him" (5:24).

But with the passing of time and the growth of population, Seth and Enoch were forgotten, and the entire pre-Flood culture (both Cainite and Sethite) began a headlong plunge into depravity in which marriage was demonized, life shortened, and violence again idolized. So we read, "The Nephilim were on the earth in those days, and also afterward, when the sons of God came in to the daughters of man and they bore children to them. These were the mighty men who were of old, the men of renown" (6:4). The phrase "mighty men" is synonymous with the word for *warriors* in Hebrew (cf. 10:8); so we understand that the "men of renown" in pre-Flood culture were violent men and that their renown came from their violence. The NIV, with its "sons of God went to the daughters," sanitizes a crude expression for sexual violence. Sexual violence was characteristic of the "men of renown," the culture's heroes.

Ultimately the culture went the way of its heroes: "Now the earth was corrupt in God's sight, and the earth was filled with violence. And God saw the earth, and behold, it was corrupt, for all flesh had corrupted their way on the earth. And God said to Noah, 'I have determined to make an end of all flesh'" (vv. 11-13). From this we learn that when a culture becomes violent ("filled with violence"), when depravity has run its course, such a culture has reached its lowest ebb and stands under imminent judgment.

Indeed, after the Flood and the destruction of all humanity except Noah and his family, God acted to curb violence by instituting capital punishment with this compelling poetic stanza:

"Whoever sheds the blood of man,
by man shall his blood be shed,
for God made man in his own image."

—9:6

Since man is created in the image of God and as such is of immense value, and since the blood (life) of man is God's alone, to take human life is to usurp God's sovereignty over life and death, thereby meriting death itself. Precisely because life is so precious, the person who willfully takes another's life must suffer death at the hands of men.

In truth, any sinful violence, even though it may not involve murder, is an assault on God's image. Unjustified violence is a crime against God. Significantly, the book of Genesis ends with an oracle against unjustified violence as the patriarchs Levi and Simeon, the perpetrators of the massacre of the Shechemites, hear their father prophesy that their descendants will be scattered among the tribes of Israel (cf. 49:5-7).

So we see that the book of Genesis unequivocally reveals God's hatred of violence and violent people. David echoes God's mind in the Psalms:

> *The Lord is in his holy temple;*
> *the LORD'S throne is in heaven;*
> *his eyes see, his eyelids test, the children of man.*
> *The LORD tests the righteous,*
> *but his soul hates the wicked and the one who loves violence.*
>
> —PSALM 11:4-5

And finally, in the New Testament the apostle Paul instances violence as the ultimate outworking of man's depravity: "Their feet are swift to shed blood; in their paths are ruin and misery, and the way of peace they have not known" (Romans 3:15-17).

Implications. This doesn't mean that violence is wrong in itself. Sometimes God himself orders violence, as for example when he directed King Saul to destroy the Amalekites and then judged Saul for not doing so (cf. 1 Samuel 15). Joshua's destruction of Ai was in direct obedience to God (cf. Joshua 8). The biblical theory of a just war involves the use of "controlled violence." Sometimes violence is a moral imperative.

Neither does the biblical teaching on violence suggest that literature depicting violence (and by extension stage and film depictions) is necessarily wrong. Violence is often essential to the telling of a story, as in *The Oxbow Incident* or the account of Gettysburg. The Bible is full of stories of violence because it is realistic literature that describes life at its worst as well as its best.[1] The Bible records infanticide, cannibalism, rape, torture, and massacre, thus demonstrating the depths of depravity to which the human race will go. Paradoxically, crucifixion, the most gruesome of accounts of violence, is also at the heart of the Bible's story of redemption. The violence of the cross teaches the most horrible and beautiful of truths—"Christ died for our sins in accordance with the Scriptures" (1 Corinthians 15:4).

What the Bible prohibits is the cultivation of a violent heart. In Scripture's language, God is opposed to "the one who loves violence" (Psalm 11:5)—those whom "violence covers . . . as a garment" (Psalm 73:6), those whose speech is violent (Proverbs 10:6, 11), and those of whom it is said, "the desire of the treacherous is for violence" (Proverbs 13:2). The Bible rejects those who glory in violence as did Lamech (Genesis 4:23-24), "the men of renown" (Genesis 6:1-8), and Simeon and Levi, whose genocidal spree earned them a curse (Genesis 49:5-7). We should note that King David, hero that he was, was not allowed to build the temple because he was a warrior and had shed blood (1 Chronicles 28:3).

In effect, the Scriptures declare an ominous "woe" to violent hearts that glory in violence and promote it in this world. There are no beatitudes for the violent. Only "Blessed are the peacemakers, for they shall be called sons of God" (Matthew 5:9).

MEDIA VIOLENCE

Violence factories. Film and television and video games stand clearly under the focus of divine judgment as unparalleled factories of violence. TV shows, films, movies edited for television, and video games expose us to a level of violence unimaginable just a few years ago, and this is especially true for children. The American Psychological Association reports that the average child watches eight thousand televised murders and a hundred thousand acts of violence before finishing *elementary school* (sixth grade). These numbers more than double by the time they graduate from high school.[2]

As to the effect of these statistics, the Parents Television Council cites a review of nearly a thousand studies presented to the American College of Forensic Psychiatry in 1998. The review of these thousand separate studies noted "that all but 18 demonstrated that screen violence leads to real violence, and that 12 of those 18 were funded by the industry."[3] A twenty-year study of four hundred children issued in 1984 by University of Illinois professors Huesman and Eron found that those who watch significant amounts of TV violence as eight-year-olds are more likely to commit violent crimes or engage in child or spouse abuse at age thirty. They concluded, "Television affects youngsters of all ages, of both genders, all socioeconomic levels and all levels of intelligence.... It cannot be denied or explained away."[4] Remember this when you hear the demurrals and prevarications of the film and TV industry.

More violent violence! Along with the frequency of violence are the graphic and horrifying depictions of violence that amount to a carnival of violence. *Die Hard 2* had a body count of 264 individual deaths! Tellingly, many people have said that when they saw September 11, they had the feeling they had seen it before in a Bruce Willis movie. Vincent Canby of the *New York Times* summarizes: "If you have the impression that movies today are bloodier and more brutal than ever in the past, and that their body counts are skyrocketing, you are absolutely right. Inflation has hit the action-adventure movie with a big slimy splat."[5] As Michael Medved says:

> The current tendency is to make mayhem a subject of mirth. As the on-screen mutilation and dismemberment become progressively more grotesque and horrible, film makers make light of their characters' pain by introducing sadistic humor as an indispensable element of entertainment.[6]

Anyone who has watched Arnold Schwarzenegger in action, dispassionately dispatching dozens of opponents in one of his major film roles, has been exposed to this cruel new notion of comedy. Even on those occasions when he isn't supposed to be playing killer robots, the Big Guy deals death with mechanical, deadpan precision; in many instances, the only twinges of humanity allowed to creep into his characterizations are those murderous *bon mots* with which he rids the world of the human rubbish arrayed against him. In *Predator* (1987), the hero impales a villain against a tree with a machete, then urges the bleeding victim to "Stick around." In a defining moment in *Total Recall* (1990), he makes use of an ascending elevator to separate the villainous Michael Ironside from both of his forearms; as Arnold is left holding the bloody stumps, all that remains of his opponent, he quips, "See you at the party."

Other leading action stars have followed Schwarzenegger's lead in trying to milk laughs from lacerations. It's the violence itself that's supposed to be hilarious, and that leaves audiences howling with laughter. A twelve-year-old girl named Betsy, interviewed after a matinee of *Total Recall*, told a reporter for *Entertainment Weekly*, "I can't say that it's violent, really. It's pretty funny to see people getting shot in the head."

The nightmarish mix of comedy and carnage demonstrates more clearly than anything else that the brutality in today's films is different in kind, not just extent, from the screen violence of the past.[7]

Manufacturing violence. The most requested article in *Christianity Today's* fifty-year history is "Trained to Kill," written by retired military psychologist Lt. Col. Dave Grossman, an expert in the psychology of killing. Col. Grossman's thesis is that the same methods used to train soldiers to kill are at work in our media and entertainment. Grossman begins by noting the established fact that the per capita murder rate doubled in the thirty-five years between 1957—when the FBI started keeping data—and 1992. He also noted that the violence rate was even higher because aggravated assault (attempting to kill someone) had risen from sixty per one hundred thousand in 1957 to over 440 per hundred thousand by 1995. And he argues that both figures would be far worse were it not for two factors: 1) the increase in the imprisonment rate of violent offenders, and 2) the vast improvement in trauma medicine learned in Vietnam. He argues that if we had the 1940-level medical technology today, the murder rate would be ten times higher.

Mr. Grossman also notes that violent crime worldwide is at a phenomenally high level. For example, in Canada per capita assaults increased almost fivefold between 1964 and 1993. Attempted murder increased almost sevenfold, and murder doubled. Europe has experienced similar statistical changes. Col. Grossman concludes:

> This virus of violence is occurring worldwide. The explanation for it has to be some new factor that is occurring in all of these countries. There are many factors involved, and none should be discounted: for example, the prevalence of guns in our society. But violence is rising in many nations with draconian gun laws. And though we should never downplay child abuse, poverty, or racism, there is only one new variable present in each of these countries, bearing the exact same fruit: media violence presented as entertainment for children.[8]

Drawing on his background as a military psychologist, the author argues convincingly that killing is unnatural—that every species has a "hardwired resistance" to killing its own kind.

Our own military history makes the point. At Gettysburg, 90 percent of the twenty-seven thousand muskets collected from the dead and dying were loaded. This is strange, because it took 95 percent of their time to load and only 5 percent to fire. And even more revealing is that over half the muskets had multiple loads in the barrels. The truth is that the average soldier would load his musket and bring it to his shoulder, but he could not bring himself to kill. So he lowered it and loaded it again. Of those who did fire, the majority fired over the enemies' heads.

In World War II, general officers' studies revealed that only 15 to 20 percent of riflemen could bring themselves to fire at an exposed enemy. Since then, the military has systematically worked at correcting the problem. By the Korean War, about 55 percent were willing to fire to kill. By Vietnam, the rate was 90 percent.[9]

The methods to achieve the willingness to kill were four:

Desensitization. In the military, the goal is to remove normal inhibitions and instill new values that embrace violence. This happens to very young children, because when they see violence, they do not have the ability to distinguish fantasy from reality. At first they are terrified, but with repeated exposures they begin to understand that viewed violence cannot hurt them. And like the rest, they soon come to view it with dispassionate nonchalance.

Classical conditioning. Such conditioning is accomplished by linking violence to pleasure, such as praise from your fellow soldiers. This happens ever so easily in the theater and home as violence is viewed and pleasure is consumed.

Operant conditioning. This conditioning is the stimulus-response procedure used to teach soldiers to shoot. Instead of a WWII bull's-eye, a human silhouette pops up into view (*stimulus*), allowing only a split second for *response.* Thought is eliminated. Only response is required. Interactive video games are the media parallel.

Role models. In the military, it's your drill sergeant. On TV, it's a person with ostensibly more muscle, more charm, more intelligence, more courage and machismo than any drill sergeant could ever possess unless portrayed on the screen.[10]

Does it work? The *Journal of the American Medical Association* said yes in its definitive 1992 study on the impact of TV violence. The research compared nations or regions that were demographically and ethnically similar. The only difference was the presence of television. In every nation, region, or city with television, there came an immediate explosion of violence on the playground, and within fifteen years a doubling of the murder rate. Why fifteen years? That's how long it takes for a three- to five-year-old to reach the "prime crime age."[11] The *Journal of the American Medical Association* concludes:

> The introduction of television in the 1950s caused a subsequent
> doubling of the homicide rate, i.e., long-term childhood exposure
> to television is a causal factor behind approximately one half of the
> homicides committed in the United States, or approximately

10,000 homicides annually. . . . If, hypothetically, television technology had never been developed, there would today be 10,000 fewer homicides each year in the United States, 70,000 fewer rapes, and 700,000 fewer injurious assaults.[12]

Woe to a culture (and its media) that celebrates violence and that elevates heroes of violence as "men of renown." Woe to those who have desensitized and conditioned (classically and operatively) and set out role models of violence. Woe to those who glory in violence. And woe to those in Christ's church who passively view it—who fail to protect their homes and their children from its degenerating effects. Woe to a church culture in which Christian young people view violence at the same rate as the rest of culture.

VOYEURISM

The dictionary definition generally limits voyeurism to seeking sexual stimulation by visual means. But here I am expanding the term to include those who through visual means derive vicarious fulfillment of any type. It is an unhealthy gaze at and preoccupation with any number of things, whether living or material, for the purpose of a thrill or sensual escape.

Violent voyeurism. Ernest Hemingway indulged in this as a bullfight aficionado. He loved the moment of death: the immense bull, thrusting and dancing with the slim figure of the matador; the glittering sword raised high in the air above the deadly horns; and finally the blade plunging deep between the animal's shoulders. Sometimes when the bull could not be killed with the sword, the matador used a short knife or puntillo. "I love to see the puntillo used," Papa would say happily. "It is exactly like turning off an electric light bulb."[13]

Hemingway's voyeuristic electricity at the fatal moment is revealing. Through visual or screen violence we can drink in pleasure in the victim's pain—and no one will know. Through the lens of a camera mounted on the gladiator's helmet we can feel how it is to kill. We can feast on the basest, most prurient depths of a dark heart. And unwittingly our souls can be devoured. We can begin to believe that violence is actually an answer to our problems.

Sexual voyeurism. The screen and now the Internet is the broad way to pornography and destruction. For many, the voyeuristic sins of the mind will provide them satisfactions that are not available in real life—because they are not Adonis and there is no Aphrodite who wants them. They become "men of renown" in the video-stained recesses of their own minds. Pathetic heroes.

Escapist voyeurism can take many forms. Celebrity voyeurism is escapist. It can be through a sports hero or a model or a movie or television star. You study him, dream of her—and in your mind you are the celebrity. The vehicles for such voyeurism are many: films, survival shows, soaps, star magazines, romance novels. Materialistic voyeurism, though it involves the inanimate, can be singularly escapist, whether it be through a catalog or a showroom. You become the possessor of what you view. Psychologists claim there is an element of possession in the obsessive viewing of something. The grand tools of voyeurism in its many forms are the media, but lesser tools include compulsive window shopping and catalog viewing.

THE BIBLE AND VOYEURISM

The answer to voyeuristic folly lies in the fact that all of us are created in the image of God. We learn this from the creation story in Genesis 1:

> *So God created man in his own image,*
> *in the image of God he created him;*
> *male and female he created them*

> —V. 27

As image-bearers of God, we can do what no other creature can do—we can hear and receive God's Word. As image-bearers, we also have the potential to rule with God in creation. Being in his image also indicates God's paternity and our filial relationship. When we, as believers, fully understand that we are in God's image, and more, that in Christ who is the very image of God we are destined for completion in his image—when we understand this and take it to heart, we will lay aside all voyeurism. Christ alone (no person or thing) is our fulfillment. Who we are in him outstrips any earthly focus. The heinous sin of violence *assaults* the image of God. The pathetic sin of voyeurism *discounts* the image of God in us.

Christians must take control of what they view. But such self-control by itself is no more than mere moralism. If we resolve to eliminate voyeurism from our lives in our own moralistic zeal, we will be doing nothing more than a good Muslim or a good Buddhist would do. And if mere bootstrap moralism becomes our method of fighting sin, there is actually no hope for us, because there is no power in us. Even hearing a sermon on the need to control what we view will do nothing apart from Christ. If we and our children are not perpetually filled with Christ and his holy Word so that they are coursing through our lives, it is all for naught. If the Bible is not taught in our homes so that it is a part of our lives, little substantial will happen.

We are not moralists; we are Christians. And as Christians, "we have the mind of Christ" (cf. 1 Corinthians 2:16). We also have the Spirit of Christ (cf. John 14:15-17). The answer to voyeurism is to become people who are filled with the riches of the Word and the mind of Christ himself. We are God's people, and now is the time.

May the mind of Christ my Savior
Live in me from day to day,
By His love and pow'r controlling
All I do and say.

May the peace of God my Father
Rule my life in everything,
That I may be calm to comfort
Sick and sorrowing.

KATE B. WILKINSON, 1925

FOR REFLECTION AND APPLICATION

• What influences in your life might be pushing you in the direction of a violent heart?

• How would you define the biblical opposite of a violent heart? How can you cultivate such a heart?

• What forms of vicarious fulfillment does our culture offer to us? Which of these are especially tempting to you? How can you resist these temptations?

NOTES

1. For more on violence in the Bible, see Leland Ryken, *Dictionary of Biblical Imagery* (Downers Grove, IL: InterVarsity Press, 1998), pp. 916-917.

2. www.babybag.com/articles/amaviol.htm, "Facts About Media Violence and Effects on the American Family," p. 1, which references the Center for Media and Public Affairs, 1992.

3. www.probe.org/does/sex-viol.html, Kerby Anderson, "Sex and Violence on Television," p. 2, citing Parents Television Council, *Special Report: What a Difference a Decade Makes*, March 30, 2000.

4. Michael Medved, *Hollywood vs. America* (New York: Harper Collins, 1992), p. 184.

5. Ibid., p. 187.

6. Ibid., p. 188.

7. Ibid., pp. 188-190.

8. *Christianity Today*, August 10, 1998,www.christianitytoday.com/ct/8t9/8t9030.html, pp. 2-3.

9. Ibid., p. 4.

10. Ibid., pp. 5-6.

11. Ibid., pp. 8-12.

12. June 10, 1992, quoted in ibid., pp. 7-8.

13. Charles Colson, *Kingdoms in Conflict* (New York/Grand Rapids, MI: William Morrow, Zondervan, 1987), p. 51.

6

Set Apart to Save:
Sexual Conduct

For this is the will of God, your sanctification: that you abstain from sexual immorality; that each one of you know how to control his own body in holiness and honor, not in the passion of lust like the Gentiles who do not know God; that no one transgress and wrong his brother in this matter, because the Lord is an avenger in all these things, as we told you beforehand and solemnly warned you. For God has not called us for impurity, but in holiness. Therefore whoever disregards this, disregards not man but God, who gives his Holy Spirit to you.

1 THESSALONIANS 4:3-8

In his book *Worldly Saints*, Leland Ryken notes, "The dominant attitude of the Catholic church throughout the Middle Ages was that sexual love itself was evil and did not cease to be so if its object was one's spouse."[1] In promoting this anti-sexual view, the ancient Roman church was heir to the mistaken understanding of the early church fathers. Tertullian and Ambrose, for example, believed that the extinction of the human race was to be preferred over against sex within marriage. St. Ambrose wrote that "married people ought to blush at the state in which they are living." Similarly, Augustine argued that the sexual relationship was innocent in marriage, but the passion that accompanies it is always sinful. He frequently counseled married couples to abstain. The medieval theologians Albertus and Aquinas likewise objected to marital intimacy because it subordinates reason to human passions.

This resulted in the Council of Trent's denunciation of those who denied that virginity was superior to the married state. Accordingly, the Roman church kept adding days in which marital sex was prohibited—until more than half the days of the year were excluded. Think of it—183 days of the year required marital abstinence. No wonder there was a Reformation!

Actually, the change *did* come through the Reformation, with its return to what the Bible actually taught. And the great heroes here were the Puritans—yes, the Puritans!—as they took on the Roman church in spirited debate. Dr. Ryken concludes: "The Puritan doctrine of sex was a watershed on the cultural history of the West. The Puritans devalued celibacy, glorified companionate marriage, affirmed married sex as both necessary and pure, established the ideal of wedded romantic love, and exalted the role of the wife."[2]

Puritan literature is filled with stunning expressions of marital love, such as the anonymous Puritan who said that when two are made one by marriage they "may joyfully give due benevolence one to the other; as two musical instruments rightly fitted do make a most pleasant and sweet harmony in a well tuned consort [concert]."[3] But it was John Milton, the great Puritan poet, who gave the most elegant expression of the biblical perspective in his description of Adam and Eve.

> *Straight side by side were laid, nor turned, I ween [imagine],*
> *Adam from his fair spouse, nor Eve the rites*
> *Mysterious of connubial love refused:*
> *Whatever hypocrites austerely talk*
> *Of purity and place and innocence,*
> *Defaming as impure what God declares*
> *Pure, and commands to some, leaves free to all.*
> *Our Maker bids increase, who bids abstain*
> *But our Destroyer, foe to God and man?*
> *Hail, wedded love. . . .*[4]

"Puritanical" an adjective for repression and grim asceticism? Hardly.

Indeed, the Bible exalts and celebrates marital sex. Adam's shout of ecstasy upon his initial sight of Eve was this, as expressed with poetic eloquence and feeling:

> *"This at last is bone of my bones*
> *and flesh of my flesh;*
> *she shall be called Woman,*
> *because she was taken out of Man."*
>
> —GENESIS 2:23

This enraptured shout represents the first human words quoted in the Bible, as well as the first poetic couplet in God's Word.

Adam's joyous cry echoes down to the present day, proclaiming the joy and intimacy of marriage. In the Genesis account, as Adam's shout subsides, the voice of Moses concludes, "Therefore a man shall leave his father and his mother and hold fast to his wife, and they shall become one flesh" (v. 24). These words become the deep well for the Bible's teaching on marriage and family.

The Bible is neither shy nor prudish about the sexual pleasures of marriage, as becomes abundantly clear in the Song of Songs. The Song of Songs is an epithalamion (wedding poem) that celebrates romantic and sexual passion within a context of marriage (marriage anticipated and then consummated).[5] It is an erotic love poem that teaches not techniques but an *attitude* about lovemaking. The portrayal of passion, though not graphic or indecent, is wholly sensuous.[6] The metaphors used encourage believers to think lovingly about the partner whom God has given them. The Song does not tell how lovers ought to kiss, but it tells what a marital kiss ought to be (cf. 1:2; 2:3; 4:11).

A dominant image in the Song is that the woman is a garden. The significance of this comes from understanding that a garden in ancient Israel was walled and private and accessible only to the owner (cf. 4:12). So we see that marital intimacy is a private thing between one man and one woman. Gardens were places of rest, refreshment, and relaxation, and the garden imagery of Song of Songs suggests the

benefits of intimacy.[7] Thus understood, the lavish lyrics of the Song
sing of *the wife* (not her body) as a garden:

> *A garden locked is my sister, my bride,*
> *a spring locked, a fountain sealed.*
> *Your shoots are an orchard of pomegranates*
> *with all choicest fruits,*
> *henna with nard,*
> *nard and saffron, calamus and cinnamon,*
> *with all trees of frankincense,*
> *myrrh and aloes,*
> *with all chief spices—*
> *a garden fountain, a well of living water,*
> *and flowing streams from Lebanon.*
>
> —SONG OF SONGS 4:12-15

How refreshing this is in a day of sexual techies with their charts and
of furrowed brows on those who lecture about technique and liberation from our Puritan inhibitions.[8]

We must also mention that both Christ and Paul go to the well of
Genesis 2. Paul, reflecting on husbands and wives being "one flesh,"
says, "This mystery is profound, and I am saying that it refers to Christ
and the church. However, let each one of you love his wife as himself,
and let the wife see that she respects her husband" (Ephesians 5:32-
33). Here is the ultimate *eros*! Loving your wife as you love yourself
means that you give everything you have of yourself to her, holding
nothing back. This is what Christ did for the church.

The lovemaking of Christians should be deep and joyous and
celebrative and lasting. *The joy of sex*, after which our culture chases
headlong, is actually a gift from God.

CULTURE'S DESECRATION

No Christian today can deny that we are living in a culture given to
the ongoing desecration of sex and marriage. As we have chronicled
at some length, sexual propagandists have taken over film and prime-

time television, so that lewdness, pornography, adultery, sexual violence, sexual humor, and double entendre occur at such a high rate that the situation can only be called an assault. Both heterosexual and homosexual fornication (a-marital sex) have been declassified from the category of sins. Often those who do not approve of unmarried sex or homosexuality are the ones represented as unhealthy, repressed souls, objects of scorn and humor. Those who protest sexual sin are characterized as shrill and retrograde.

And the desecration of the sacred is deepening as a chic pedophilia is being promoted in a number of places—therapeutic, literary, and academic. Mainstream publishing houses, journals, magazines, and bookstores now carry the propaganda of "adult-child love."[9] Even bestiality has its elite proponents, such as Princeton professor Peter Singer's propagandistic review of Midas Dekker's *Dearest Pet: On Bestiality*.[10]

But apart from the slide into perversion, the effect of the ongoing desecration has been a reductionist view of sex. The magnificent, multidimensional marital sexuality of the Bible has been shrinkwrapped into a flat-sided, single-dimensioned, materialist package. Wendy Shalit, in her important book *A Return to Modesty*, surveys the results of a generation raised on casual sex. Sex on campus, she explains, is about as personal as "two airplanes refueling." In fact, the current phrase is "hooking up." At the heart of the idea is that the liaison is based solely on physical attraction and implies no suggestion of attachment. Subsequently, a woman should not expect to be called or dated after a sexual encounter.[11]

Key to this reductionist view of sex is the regarding of sex as essentially a skill. Jenell Williams Paris, professor of anthropology at Bethel College, notes that the media's thirty-something sitcoms portray sexuality as a trait separate from relationship, separate from character, and separate from commitment. She says:

> Similarly, masters of technique are shown as the best sexual partners, while virgins, awkward lovers, or people with sexual dysfunction make for great humor. Even nonsexual things like clothes,

food, and music become subjects for sexual innuendoes, joking, and arousal. If sex isn't easy for you, or if you think too hard about sexual choices, something must be comically wrong with you.[12]

Sex has been reduced to the level of the Discovery Channel.

Yet paradoxically, this reductionistic sex is held on the level of "religion" in general culture. As Malcolm Muggeridge said, "Sex is the mysticism of a materialist society, with its own mysteries—that is my birth control pill; swallow it in remembrance of me! and its own sacred texts and scripture—the erotica that fall like black atomic rain on the just and unjust alike, drenching us, blinding us, stupefying us. To be carnally minded is life!"[13]

The sexual wreckage clutters our culture's landscape. In few places is it more evident than the pornography industry. Cyber-smut is one of the few profitable e-commerce sectors. Online stock trading is the other sector, but its typical profit margins are about 0.2 percent, compared to porn site profits that often reach 30 percent.[14] The porn sites are growing. According to *U.S. News and World Report,* Nielsen NetRatings for January 2000 showed a 40 percent increase in porn site traffic compared with four months earlier.[15] *Crain's Chicago Business* (November 5, 2001) quotes *Playboy Magazine's* Christie Hefner as referencing their website as the reason they will show profits next year.

The toll of pornography among Christians and the leadership of the church is unexpected and disheartening. In August 2000 *Christianity Today* conducted an exclusive survey of its readership, both lay and clergy, regarding Internet pornography. The good news was that 67 percent of the clergy and 64 percent of the laity had never visited a sexually explicit website. The bad news was that 33 percent of the clergy and 36 percent of the laity *had.* Of those who had visited a pornographic website, half the clergy said they had visited the sites a few times in the previous year, as compared to about 40 percent of the lay respondents. Some 18 percent of the third of the clergy who had visited sexually explicit websites were revisiting them several times a month.[16]

So there we have it: Roughly one-third of pastors have visited a pornographic website, and about 16 percent did so several times a year, and about 5 percent do it frequently. And these are *CT*-reading pastors who, notwithstanding their anonymity, were *willing* to answer the survey. I wonder what the statistics are among the general clergy and laity if the truth were known. Substantially higher, I think.

The reasons for this are three: *accessibility, anonymity,* and *affordability*. Pornography is just a click away, and no one will know who is visiting. The visitor is faceless and nameless. And it is cheap. There are pastors and Christian leaders who would never visit an adult bookstore or rent explicit videos but who are now downloading images and watching live streaming video in the privacy of their homes and offices.[17]

If this is true of the leadership, how much more is it true of the average church attender? Perhaps the letter that I received from a church member gives some indication. He writes:

> My question to you on Sunday was whether you would be covering the Internet in more detail. The reason I asked is that I've been somewhat surprised that I have not heard this issue covered more from the pulpit and in Christian media. I'm probably more sensitized to this issue than most because I spend 40 hours a week developing Internet technologies to enable businesses to more effectively use the web, and I see the Internet as a very powerful and useful tool. However, I'm also deeply concerned about the avenues for decadent content that have been opened into the home.
>
> I'm fortunate to have many good Christian male friends that I can confide in and talk openly with about their faith and areas in their life where they are struggling. What has been alarming to me is that out of a dozen or so close friends that I have talked to, all but one has admitted that they struggle in this area and frequently fail. All of these friends are very committed followers of Christ, many involved in full-time Christian service. What I see is that Christians who would have never even considered going into an adult store, renting an R/X rated movie, or dialing a 900 number are now continually failing in this area because of the anonymity and free and easy access to this type of content on the Internet. What is worse, is seeing the grip and pull it has on people once they start down this path.

> Based on my experience, the Internet has become Satan's number one tool in the 21st century and it seems to be a more silent infection into the body of believers because it typically only involves the user and his computer.

I think that the problem is bigger than we know. I do know this: One out of eight pastors commits adultery while in the ministry, and one out of four Christian men are likewise guilty.[18] I also know that the divorce rates for Christians and non-Christians are virtually the same.

As to pornography, I know that it makes the viewer a pathetic voyeur. I know that it is a sin against one's wife and demeans her. I know that it is adultery, as Jesus explained: "But I say to you that everyone who looks at a woman with lustful intent has already committed adultery with her in his heart. If your right eye causes you to sin, tear it out and throw it away. For it is better that you lose one of your members than that your whole body be thrown into hell" (Matthew 5:28-29). I know that pornography provides a false intimacy and pseudo-fulfillment that puts tremendous strain on marriages. I know that it provides a false sense of acceptance. I know that it weakens the church. How can the pulpit have power if the preacher is a voyeur? How can our prayers have power if we regard sin in our hearts? How can our children respect us when our inner ethos betrays us? How can we preach Christ to a sensual world when we too are in the grip of sensuality? Our power, our spiritual leverage, rests on our being distinct from the world, in Christ. The holiness of Jesus Christ must characterize our lives if we wish to declare Christ's glory among the nations.

THE CHURCH'S CALL

Here is God's will and God's call for every one of us:

> *For this is the will of God, your sanctification: that you abstain from sexual immorality; that each one of you know how to control his own body in holiness and honor, not in the passion of lust like the Gentiles who do not know God; that no one transgress and wrong his brother*

in this matter, because the Lord is an avenger in all these things, as we told you beforehand and solemnly warned you. For God has not called us for impurity, but in holiness. Therefore whoever disregards this, disregards not man but God, who gives his Holy Spirit to you.

—1 THESSALONIANS 4:3-8

If the reading of this passage is not convincing enough concerning the biblical call, we must understand that it is based on Leviticus 19:2, where God says, "You shall be holy, for I the LORD your God am holy"—a command that is given in the context of warning against sexual sin. To reject this is to sin against the Holy Spirit—the living presence of God who is speaking right now, as the Thessalonian passage makes so clear. To reject this call to sexual purity is to reject God.

Corporate call. We are called as a church to create a culture that nurtures purity. We must carefully guard our hearts. Here is Job's wisdom: "I have made a covenant with my eyes; how then could I gaze at a virgin?" (Job 31:1). Here is wisdom from Proverbs: "Can a man carry fire next to his chest and his clothes not be burned?" (6:27). Here is Jesus' wisdom: "And if your eye causes you to sin, tear it out. It is better for you to enter the kingdom of God with one eye than with two eyes to be thrown into hell" (Mark 9:47). Here is Paul's wisdom: "But sexual immorality and all impurity or covetousness must not even be named among you, as is proper among saints. Let there be no filthiness nor foolish talk nor crude joking, which are out of place, but instead let there be thanksgiving" (Ephesians 5:3-4).

We must begin marriage with a covenantal oath, and then never break our oath. Marriage portrays Christ and the church. As the husband and wife are physically united as one, Christ and the church are spiritually one. The way we live reflects on Christ and the church. We do not have the luxury of being able to say nothing about the church. Our lives always speak. Mental and physical infidelity lies to the world about the spiritual faithfulness of Jesus and his people.[19] Immorality trashes the mystery of Christ and his church. It desecrates the holy.

In cultivating purity in the church, no tactic is more important than celebrating and elevating marriage. Apart from Scripture's call, the greatest argument for sexual purity is the living example of a faithful man and woman deeply in love. This is what our cyber-sexed, reductionist world must see. And more, they must see that Christ is the center of marriage and the answer to sexual immorality.

The church must exercise spiritual discipline in respect to sensual purity and marriage. It must do so with an eye to restoration and the glory of Christ.

Individual call. The corporate call to purity and loving fidelity in the home is also, of course, an individual call. The home is the place where we can and must protect our families. We have already considered what we ought to do regarding film and TV. But what can be done about the Internet? The answer is similar to what I have already recommended in regard to sensuality on television, but the following specific applications to the Internet needs to be stated:

• You must pray for the Holy Spirit's help in bringing conviction of sin, and then for his empowering you to forsake your sins.

• You must ask the question as to whether you really need access to the Internet in your home. It is significant that there are Internet professionals who will not allow it in their homes for security reasons, not to mention the dangers of access to morally dangerous material.

• If you consider the Internet a necessity, you must build in a system of accountability. There are helpful software programs, but all are relatively easy to bypass. The most effective protection is a monitoring software that logs the websites and the destinations of e-mail. Give your spouse the password so she or he can monitor where you've been. Sit down regularly with your children, and review the family's Internet activity.

• Your computers should be kept in open places in the house. They should not be in bedrooms.

• If you or a member of your family is being victimized by cyber-porn, you must see your pastor immediately. Confession and repentance are not enough. There are also a number of website ministries that can be of help (see Appendix II).

In all of this, the ultimate answer is Christ himself. There are two things that we must take to heart. First, the Christian life is a marriage to Christ. He is the groom, and we, the church, are his bride. He has been and always will be faithful to us. He has given his life for us. His goal is to present us to the Father without blemish, holy and blameless. Jesus is our sanctification (cf. 1 Corinthians 1:30). He will do it. So in all our concern for purity we must look to Christ.

Second, we must also remember that while the Christian life is marriage *to* Christ, Christian marriage is also union *in* Christ. As a couple, when you and your spouse celebrate and lift up your marriage to him, you both will draw closer to one another. As you allow his marital love to fill you, you will better love your spouse. As you invite his purity to course through your soul, you will know how to control your own body. And your marriage will be a garden of delight.

FOR REFLECTION AND APPLICATION

• How does our culture's desecration of sexuality, as well as its sexual idolatry, actually pervert God's intention in creating us as sexual beings?

• How might this cultural desecration pervert sex within marriage?

• How might your church respond to the corporate call to create a church that nurtures sexual purity?

• How can you and your family respond to the individual call to loving sexual fidelity and purity in the home and in personal life?

• What specific steps will you take toward healthy, biblical discipline in this area?

NOTES

1. Leland Ryken, *Worldly Saints* (Grand Rapids, MI: Zondervan, 1986), pp. 40-41 is the source for the information shared here on Roman Catholic sexual asceticism.

2. Ibid., p. 53.

3. Ibid., p. 44.

4. Ibid., pp. 53-54.

5. Frederic C. Putnam, "Sexual Relations as Redeemed Intimacy: The

Message of the Song of Solomon," *Modern Reformation*, Vol. 10, No. 6, November/December 2001, pp. 23, 27.

6.   For more on the Song of Solomon as a collection of love poems, see Leland Ryken, *Words of Delight: A Literary Introduction to the Bible* (Grand Rapids, MI: Baker, 1992), pp. 271-289. Also excellent is Douglas Wilson, *Reforming Marriage* (Moscow, ID: Canon Press, 1995), pp. 102-103.

7.   Putnam, "Sexual Relations as Redeemed Intimacy," p. 26.

8.   Wilson, *Reforming Marriage*, pp. 104-105 writes: "The liberated Modern, with the furrowed brow of a frustrated technocrat, wants to talk about the various positions of sexual engineering, accompanied by charts, diagrams, and technical manuals—along with stern and graphic lectures to all us repressed Puritans."

9.   Mary Eberstadt, "Pedophilia Chic Reconsidered," *The Weekly Standard*, January 1/January 8, 2001, p. 19.

10. www.nationalreview._com/nr_comment 030501a.shtmal, Kathryn Jean Lopez, "Peter Singer Strikes Again," March 15, 2001, pp. 1-3.

11. Wendy Shalit, *A Return to Modesty* (New York: Free Press, 1999), pp. 27-30.

12. Jenell Williams Paris, "The Truth About Sex," *Christianity Today*, November 12, 2001, p. 13.

13. Malcolm Muggeridge, *Confessions of a Twentieth-century Pilgrim* (San Francisco: Harper and Row, 1988), Chapter 7.

14. "We've Got Porn," *Christianity Today*, June 12, 2000, p. 13.

15. Ibid.

16. "Tangled in the Worst of the Web," *Christianity Today*, March 5, 2001, pp. 4-5.

17. Ibid., p. 6.

18. "How Common Is Pastoral Indiscretion?," *Leadership*, Winter 1988, p. 12 says:

> The survey probed the frequency of behavior that pastors themselves feel is inappropriate. Since you have been in local church ministry, have you ever done anything with someone (not your spouse) that you feel was sexually inappropriate? The responses: 23 per cent yes; 77 percent no. The "inappropriate" behavior was left undefined—possibly ranging from unguarded words to flirtation to adultery. Subsequent questions were more specific. Have you ever had sexual

intercourse with someone other than your spouse since you have been in local-church ministry? Yes: 12 percent. No: 88 percent. And of that 88 percent, many indicated their purity had not come easily.

To lend some perspective to these figures, CTi researchers also surveyed almost one thousand subscribers of *Christianity Today* magazine who are *not* pastors. Incidences of immorality were nearly double: 45 percent indicated having done something they considered sexually inappropriate, 23 percent said they had had extramarital intercourse, and 28 percent said they had engaged in other forms of extramarital sexual contact.

19. Wilson, *Reforming Marriage*, p. 106.

7

Set Apart to Save: Modesty

But put on the Lord Jesus Christ, and make no provision for the flesh, to gratify its desires.

ROMANS 13:14

While the subject of sexual conduct discussed in the preceding chapter concerns more men, the focus of this chapter on modesty has more to say to women (especially younger women). Of course women would not dress immodestly if men did not create an ethos that encourages them in that direction.

My wife records her dismay at our current situation with these words:

If you are blind or from another planet, you may conceivably have missed the fact that modesty has disappeared. It is dead and buried! If you don't think so, go shopping with a teenager. The fashion gurus have made sure that every item of clothing today's teen girl might need was designed to provoke thoughts that are other than virginal. It calls to mind the prophet Jeremiah's exclamation: "Are they ashamed of their loathsome conduct? No, they have no shame at all; they do not even know how to blush" (Jeremiah 6:15).[1]

My wife is not alone in her frustration. This is the sentiment of most mothers (especially Christian mothers) in regard to their daughters. Even someone as "out of it" as I am gets slapped with the realization of where our culture has gone in regard to immodesty. I recently took a shortcut through an Abercrombie & Fitch store, where I saw mural-sized photos of young men and women that were evocative of the frescoes of Pompeii. Presumably the murals were meant to sell clothing, though the models were wearing little of it.

One of my colleagues' wives tuned in to the Victoria's Secret Christmas special to give me the flavor of the much-promoted event. What she saw were top models in underwear and angel wings striding across the stage to the backdrop and music of a swaying gospel choir—a choreographed erotic desecration of Christianity and Christmas. Let's see: erotic underwear, angel wings for Christmas angels, and a gospel choir ostensibly singing about the good news of Christ. What a laugh the secular Hollywood establishment must have had at the juxtapositioning. But heaven isn't laughing. Someday, apart from God's grace, there will be weeping and grinding of teeth.

Immodesty has invaded everyday conversation. As my wife notes, "We all have had the experience of pouring ourselves a cup of coffee and sitting down in front of the TV for a little diversion, clicking to a talk show, and hearing the host question a woman about her sex life. The exchange is degrading and frankly embarrassing. So we flip to another channel, and there to our amazement we hear couples revealing painful family secrets. We change the channel only to view a discussion with young girls and their mothers. The mothers are defending their daughters' rights to dress indecently!"[2] In disgust, we turn off the smorgasbord of sexual swill. Today girls are sometimes as profane and sexually frank as stereotypical males. Both freely use expletive-laced language and filthy vocabulary to describe body parts—degrading what a holy, good God has made. It all seems very hip and liberated. Actually, it's the vocabulary of slavery.

Modern dance moves imitate sexual intercourse. But they are as old as Babylon. Even workouts become sensual events—males and females together pumping iron, sweating together in the cloying aroma of estrogen and testosterone—effecting a casual hands-on intimacy proper only for husbands and wives. The mystery is gone.

What Fuels Immodesty

As to what fuels immodesty, there are several factors, most of which require the designation "business" or "industry."

The fashion industry. Early on, Calvin Klein led the way in promoting a drugged-out cocaine chic as pale, skinny adolescent men and women posed in jeans (some with flies unzipped) in various postures of strung-out languor. Today Abercrombie & Fitch is the leader in marketing lewdness. At the heart of their marketing strategy is their quarterly catalog, for which the company charges customers and requires proof that the buyers are at least eighteen—a sure way to make younger customers want to find a way to get it. Catalogs like "Naughty and Nice" are light on the nice, with suggestive poses, provocative group photos, and interviews with porn stars. Of course, the catalog sells out.[3]

Abercrombie & Fitch is at the extreme of an ever-increasing sensual curve for which the dollar is the bottom line. And many labels are feeling the degenerating pull of its sexual gravity. It's particularly hard for young women to find clothing that is stylish and not degrading. Even sizing has become pernicious—so that what is now labeled "large" is equivalent to what was once "small." No one wants to be large. So guess what?

The body industry. If anything trumps the fashion industry in promoting immodesty, it's the body industry. The body business lives on the promotion of the myth that you cannot be happy without the body you desire, and you can have the body you want through diet and exercise. Never mind the realities of genetics— that you were born with a God-given body type as a mesomorph, ectomorph, or endomorph—because you can be "morphed." Never mind, because disciplined diet and exercise will change you into a god in your own image. The industry pours untold billions into perpetuating the myth.

Professional model Owen McKibben puts the phone down slowly. He is facing a daunting mission. McKibben has just learned that he has less than three months to prepare for a cover shoot for *Men's Health* magazine. Although he is already in Olympic-grade condition, he's not buff enough! His abdominals must be perfected. So for three grueling months he eats almost all protein, ingests virtually no sugar, and "goes for it"—punishing his abs, pumping weights, running "stadiums," and doing incessant pull-ups and leg raises— until finally his body fat is less than 7 percent and every muscle and vein bulges under his professionally tanned skin. He's ready.

As the sun rises over Miami's Biscayne Bay, he's striding across the sand toward the shoot, followed by a gaggle of twenty-four editors, extra models, a camera crew, stylists, photographers, assistant photographers, drivers, and a pair of Miami police officers. The focus is on McKibben and especially his abs as he kneels in the surf throwing handfuls of water in the air and laughing silently for the camera. After multiple poses in various locations, after twelve hours of waiting for the right wave and sunlight to dramatize his physique, the shoot is over. From some six thousand photos, one will be singled out—and Mr. McKibben's abs will be divine.

After this, the editor-in-chief of *Men's Health* will spend a full week obsessing about the cover, choosing from over thirty mock-up versions. "Readers have to want to be the guy on the cover," he says.[4] The magazine's cover carries a variation of "Incredible abs in just three weeks." All you need to do is buy *Men's Health* and follow the directions. And with those abs you'll have a rich, full life.

Of course the same thing has been going on for years with big-budget women's magazines like *Vogue, Glamour, Harper's Bazaar, Vanity Fair,* and *Mademoiselle.* But the effect upon women has become even more oppressive than upon men—especially Gen X women. According to Barbara Dafoe Whitehead, the reason for this lies in feminism's so-called girlhood project and its declaration of war on what feminists viewed as Victorian double standards for boys and girls. They demanded that boys and girls be raised in a unified manner modeled on traditional boyhood. So in play and pursuits girls were encouraged to imitate boys. The copy-the-boys approach led to increased participation in sports, in itself an involvement with many benefits. But the downside has become females' discontent and unhappiness about their bodies. The tomboy ideal is impossibly demanding. Some girls are naturally lithe and wiry, but most are not. The praises sung to tiny Olympic gymnasts and skaters instills inferiority and body hatred. And the fashion magazines that girls begin to read at ages nine or ten, and read into their twenties, enhance body shame. Dr. Whitehead concludes:

> Girls respond to body shame with rigid technocratic monitoring of their bodies. Again, the strenuous pursuit of feminine virtue has not disappeared but shifted location. The virtue of staying sexually pure has been replaced by the virtue of staying physically fit. . . . It does not take a degree in cultural anthropology to figure out that more is going on here than mere exercise. In girl culture today, "working out" is the new self-purification ritual, deeply invested with positive moral meaning. Good girls work out. Bad girls let themselves go. In the same way, eating has become a means of self-purification, and food itself has been moralized.[5]

So today high school and college students are in the midst of an epidemic of anorexia and other sorts of modesty-related disorders.

The beauty industry. Immodesty is fueled by an inordinate emphasis on the body and on the myth that you can't be happy in a less than perfect body—which you can have through disciplined diet and exercise. This culturally induced delusion and frustration is further fueled by the fashion industry's peddling of fashions for skinny models who epitomize the ideal. Fashion's impossible, immodest clothes leave most young women intimidated—confused and helpless prey for the beauty industry.

The beauty industry feeds on these insecurities, selling implants, liposuction, plastic surgeries, collagen injections, drugs, and every kind of lipstick, eye shadow, shampoo, dye, emollient, cream, soap, cleanser, enhancer, perfume, conditioner, and exfoliant that the commercial mind can imagine.

Sin's industry. And then there is sin's industry—that is, our own sin's industriousness in dragging us down into immodesty. At the heart of our sin is self-love. We are naturally lovers of self rather than lovers of God. We are naturally self-focused rather than other-focused. We readily succumb to sinful pride. Pride fuels immodesty.

The combined influences of the body industry, the clothing industry, the beauty industry, and sin's industry produce an emphasis on external appearance alone. These immense pressures serve to marginalize modesty, until finally it is viewed as a quaint sentiment of a bygone day.

EFFECTS OF IMMODESTY

Immodesty in effect chips away the protective wall around a woman's life that is meant to make her a pleasurable garden, as in the Song of Songs. Instead of being "a garden locked," "a spring locked" (Song 4:12), she is not private, and her pleasures are diminished.

Immodesty demystifies. Immodesty diminishes the mystery of sexuality. Peggy Noonan convincingly argues that the modesty of the 1950s made sex sexier.[6] Wendy Shalit, in her best-selling book *A Return to Modesty*, writes, "Certainly sexual modesty may damp down superficial allure, the kind of allure that inspires a one-night stand. But the kind of allure that lasts—that is what modesty protects and inspires. Modesty damps down crudeness; it doesn't damp down Eros. In fact, it is more likely to enkindle it."[7] "Modesty is Cupid's faithful bodyguard" (Arial Swartly). Modesty perpetuates the delicious mystery.

Immodesty devalues. Every culture protects and fences in what it most values. Immodesty removes the protection and promotes a devaluation of sexuality and marriage. When a woman's worth is determined by her visual appeal, she is reduced to an object. Her value is determined in a way akin to livestock at the county fair.

Immodesty is demeaning both to the onlooker and the one looked upon.

Immodesty breeds shallowness. Immodesty communicates that "this is all there is to me." It suggests a superficial, flat-dimensioned soul. It invites shallow exchange. It promotes temporary relationship.

Immodesty tempts. Immodesty is proverbially associated with temptation. Within the Christian community, immodesty regularly causes others (especially brothers) to stumble. Most adolescent girls don't have a clue about how the mind of a young man works! Sisters in Christ, especially younger ones, should take care not to dress in a way that leads their brothers to engage in lustful thinking leading to improper behavior. There should be a mutual concern for one another's souls.

Immodesty confuses. Our culture's immodesty places huge stress on young women. No one wants to be "out of it" or thought weird. So some young Christians simply refuse to face the problem and instead conform to provocative styles. Others work it through and dress modestly without compromise. And still others react to the pressure by dressing down in unbecoming lumberjack style rather than thinking through what is feminine and unprovocative.

These are tough days for everyone, especially young women who desire to lead a modest, chaste life. The pressures toward immodesty are pervasive and complex. Foremost is an immodest culture with its immodest dress pushed by its powerful purveyors from Victoria's Secret to Abercrombie & Fitch and their unprincipled drive for the bottom line. All this is served with the swill of immodest language in smutty street talk and urbane vulgarities and is acted out in basely immodest behavior consonant with the orgiastic culture of darkness.

Thus the cultural engines that fuel immodesty are immense: the fashion industry, the body industry, the beauty industry, and sin's industry—all living off each other in dark symbiosis, promoting an immodesty that at once demystifies, devalues, makes superficial, tempts, and confuses. These are indeed tough times for the modest.

THE BIBLE ON MODESTY

The Christian's only hope is in Christ and his Holy Word. And for the man or woman who has been victimized by the propaganda of the body industry, the answer is that you have been created in the image of God, and as such you are a beautiful and unique creation by God—whether tall or short, skinny or unskinny, well-endowed or less endowed, muscular or muscle-less. You must come to see this like Carla Barnhill did during her high school years. As she tells it:

> One night, when I was in one of my usual "I hate me" funks, I rode my bike around town for an hour or so hoping the night air would cheer me up a little. I ended up at the playground of my elementary school. I got off my bike and sat on a swing.
>
> It was a clear spring night with no clouds, a full moon and a sky bursting with stars. As I sat on the swing, I looked up at the spectacular sky and thought about how amazing God's creation is. And it hit me. *Yes, the sky is beautiful. Yes, the trees are beautiful and the mountains and the oceans and all of God's earth. But in God's eyes, I am more precious, more valuable, more beautiful than any of it.*
>
> For the first time in years, I thought about myself from God's perspective. In my mind, I imagined God in his little workshop crafting me by hand—choosing just the right shade of brown for my eyes, the right shape for my hands, the perfect amount of curl for my hair. And then I imagined him watching me day after day as I looked in the mirror and criticized how he had made me.
>
> God had put me together with love and pride. His love for me was more enormous than I could possibly grasp. And in spite of all that, I had the nerve to think he'd messed up.
>
> I ran to my bike, rushed home and scrambled up to my room. I flipped to the Psalms for a chapter I remembered that spoke of the glory of nature. There it was, Psalm 104, a psalm celebrating God's incredible creation. As I read it, I kept thinking, *Look at how amazing creation is. Look at how much care God took in making this world, and he's sharing it with you, Carla.*

As I fell asleep that night, I felt something I hadn't felt in a very long time. I felt peace and contentment with myself. I knew that I was one of God's most amazing creations and that to doubt it, even for a second, was an insult to God.[8]

Having understood our identity and eternal worth before God just as he made us, there is an especially elevating directive to women: "Likewise also that women should adorn themselves in respectable apparel, with modesty and self-control, not with braided hair and gold or pearls or costly attire, but with what is proper for women who profess godliness—with good works" (1 Timothy 2:9-10). "With modesty and self-control" is synonymous with the word *chaste*. To be chaste primarily means to refrain from acts or desires that are not virginal or not sanctioned by marriage vows. Dressing modestly means wearing clothes that do not arouse thoughts or actions that promote sensuality. This is God's will for all women.

God's women must begin with their hearts, allowing God's Word to search out the thoughts and intentions that influence how they dress. They must turn their attention to the beauties God values most—beauties that have little to do with clothing.

The apostle Peter points the way to this beauty, saying, "Do not let your adorning be external—the braiding of hair, the wearing of gold, or the putting on of clothing—but let your adorning be the hidden person of the heart with the imperishable beauty of a gentle and quiet spirit, which in God's sight is very precious" (1 Peter 3:3-4). Such beauty does not rely on external helps; it is deeply rooted in faith and trust in God. It is a beauty that grows as our hearts respond in ongoing surrender to God's will for us. Each time we act in obedience to God's Word and will for us, we experience an amazing renewal: "Though our outer nature is wasting away, our inner nature is being renewed day by day" (2 Corinthians 4:16).

The Bible likens the application of God's Word to our lives to the act of dressing. So as we follow God's directive, it is good to visualize ourselves "putting on" the good things of God.

Put on the new self, created after the likeness of God in true righteousness and holiness.

—EPHESIANS 4:24

Put on the whole armor of God, that you may be able to stand against the schemes of the devil.

—EPHESIANS 6:11

. . . put on the new self, which is being renewed in knowledge after the image of its creator.

—COLOSSIANS 3:10

The night is far gone; the day is at hand. So then let us cast off the works of darkness and put on the armor of light.

—ROMANS 13:12

Put on then, as God's chosen ones, holy and beloved, compassion, kindness, humility, meekness, and patience, bearing with one another and, if one has a complaint against another, forgiving each other; as the Lord has forgiven you, so you also must forgive. And above all these put on love, which binds everything together in perfect harmony.

—COLOSSIANS 3:12-14

. . . put on your strength, O Zion; put on your beautiful garments.

—ISAIAH 52:1

Clothe yourselves, all of you, with humility toward one another.

—1 PETER 5:5

But put on the Lord Jesus Christ, and make no provision for the flesh, to gratify its desires.

—ROMANS 13:14

Women should adorn themselves . . . with what is proper for women who profess godliness—with good works.

—1 TIMOTHY 2:9-10

When such are our garments, we all will be clothed in modesty. A great "yes" to God here is the answer for a godly, chaste life.

Modesty is the entire church's responsibility. We together must create a culture in which modesty flourishes. There must be a place where women are safe and accepted for who they are rather than for what they look like. It must also be a place that encourages and models feminine modesty. It must be a place where all learn to clothe themselves with the character of Christ.

Parents must take back the responsibility for modesty. You can't expect someone who has lived only fourteen or fifteen years on this earth to know when and where to draw the line. Certainly some of your daughters can do it, but most will need your help.

Fathers, you are essential to how your daughters regard themselves. Years ago I knew a father of several daughters who had an eye for women other than his wife. He verbally admired other women in front of his wife and daughters, freely commenting on their beauties. Thus he sowed bitter seeds of immodesty in his daughters. They knew what their father valued. And they lived it out.

Men and young men, guard your eyes and your hearts. Job's wisdom will stand you well: "I have made a covenant with my eyes; how then could I gaze at a virgin?" (Job 31:1). You may not be able to avoid the first look, but you can avoid the second. Develop the discipline of never taking that second look. Women will know if you do. They know where your eyes go. Develop modest eyes.

The culture of modesty—the culture of respect. Holy eyes and holy hearts. These are the souls that God is pleased to use to spread the Good News.

FOR REFLECTION AND APPLICATION

• What are some attitudes or behaviors that point to an excessive self-focus on the body?

• What are the leading causes of these attitudes or behaviors?

• What is the impact of immodesty on healthy sexuality and intimacy?

• According to the following Scripture passages, with what kind of clothing is God most concerned?
  • Ephesians 4:24
  • Ephesians 6:11
  • Colossians 3:10, 12-14
  • Romans 13:12, 14
  • Isaiah 52:1
  • 1 Peter 3:3-4; 5:5

NOTES

1. Barbara Hughes, *Disciplines of a Godly Woman* (Wheaton, IL: Crossway Books, 2001), pp. 92-93.

2. Ibid., p. 89.

3. Christi Parsons, "Catalogue War Puts Wood in Spotlight," *Chicago Tribune*, July 22, 2001.

4. Alex Kuczynski, cover story, "Oh, How Far a Magazine Will Go to Stimulate Newsstand Sales," *New York Times*, Monday, June 18, 2001.

5. "The Girls of Gen X," *The American Enterprise*, January/February 1998, Vol. 9, No. 1, pp. 55-56.

6. Peggy Noonan, "You'd Cry Too If It Happened to You," *Forbes*, September 14, 1992, p. 68:

    You know what else I bet he thought, though he didn't say it. It was a more human world in that it was a sexier world, because sex was still a story. Each high school senior class had exactly one girl who got pregnant and one guy who was the father, and it was the town's annual scandal. Either she went somewhere and had the baby and put it up for adoption, or she brought it home as a new baby sister, or the couple got married and the town topic changed. It was a stricter, tougher society, but its bruising sanctions came from ancient wisdom.

7. Wendy Shalit, *A Return to Modesty* (New York: The Free Press, 1999), pp. 172-173.

8. Carla Barnhill, "Ugly Me," *Campus Life*, July/August 1999, Vol. 58, No. 1, pp. 34-37.

8

Set Apart to Save: Pluralism

For God so loved the world, that he gave his only Son, that whoever believes in him should not perish but have eternal life. For God did not send his Son into the world to condemn the world, but in order that the world might be saved through him. Whoever believes in him is not condemned, but whoever does not believe is condemned already, because he has not believed in the name of the only Son of God.

JOHN 3:16-18

Six weeks after the September 11 terrorist attacks, Rev. Robert Schuller, minister of the 10,000-member Crystal Cathedral, sat in a Villa Park, Illinois, mosque with Louis Farrakhan and Iman Wallace Deen Mohammed. Schuller was on tour to promote his new autobiography *My Journey*. But after September 11 he said, "I wanted to have evenings of hope." The event was interfaith, with Muslims, Christians, Jews, and Sikhs in attendance. As the *Chicago Tribune* reported it:

> For decades, Schuller said, he was a proponent of the kind of proselytizing that pushed Muslims to become Christians. Then he realized that asking people to change their faith was "utterly ridiculous." . . . Schuller's first interaction with a Muslim group came four years ago, when Mohammed invited him to give the opening sermon at the Muslim American Society's New Jersey convention. And in 1999, he was asked by the grand mufti of Syria to preach in Damascus. "When I met the grand mufti . . . I sensed the presence of God," he wrote in his autobiography. The two

men, he said, focused on similarities, not differences. . . . "The purpose of religion is not to say, 'I have all the answers, and my job is to convert you.' That road leads to the Twin Towers. That attitude is an invitation to extremists," he said. After Sept. 11, he said, the emphasis should move from proselytizing "to just trying to help everybody who had hurts and hopes."[1]

Amazing! Robert Schuller, an ordained Christian clergyman, credits Christian attempts at evangelism and missions as being responsible for September 11—an assertion that is historically and politically naive and theologically brain-dead. Significantly, Dr. Schuller's words received slight attention in the popular press, either kudos or critiques. What he said was not particularly newsworthy, despite the fact that he had departed from the historic position of Christianity of some twenty centuries. Schuller's remarks were politically correct to the nth degree. He had simply gone with the pluralistic flow.

Now consider Franklin Graham's remarks two weeks later during an NBC interview: "We're not attacking Islam, but Islam has attacked us"; "The God of Islam is not the same God. He's not the son of God of the Christian or Judeo-Christian faith. It's a different God, and I believe it is a very evil and wicked religion."[2]

Also recall the journalistic firestorm that followed. NBC gave Graham the opportunity to retract his words and was shocked when he refused. No doubt Franklin Graham's tone and remarks could have been better worded and more nuanced. But what he said is consonant with the position of the apostolic church and the medieval church in both its Roman Catholic and Orthodox expressions and, since the Reformation, of Protestants, Orthodox believers, and Catholics down through the nineteenth century. While the followers of Mohammed may display various levels of human goodness and human evil, the religion itself rejects the divinity of Christ and Christ's substitutionary atonement—and thus bases its theology on a wicked blasphemy. Such a view rides on evil—which God will judge.

In a subsequent *Wall Street Journal* interview entitled "My View of Islam," Graham roundly defended himself, pointing to the tens of millions of dollars his organization (Samaritan's Purse) has given in relief to Muslims, saying:

> I do not believe Muslims are evil people because of their faith. I personally have many Muslim friends. But I decry the evil that has been done in the name of Islam, or any other faith—including Christianity. I agree with President Bush that as a country we are at war with terrorists, not with Islam. But as a minister, not a politician, I believe it is my responsibility to speak out against the terrible deeds that are committed as a result of Islamic teaching.[3]

And then he went on to catalog Islam's treatment of women and the homicidal violence toward those who attempt to convert from Islam. In most Islamic countries it is a crime to build a Christian church.

Am I picking on Islam? Not at all. I only use it because its recent high profile and the shocked response to any who would criticize it is illustrative of the intransigent, entrenched philosophical pluralism of our day—not to mention the popular press's theological ignorance.

Today's pluralism holds that all religions are equally true. It sees the world as a religious garden through which we can wander, plucking the flowers that smell sweetest to us. The ultimate test of what is authentic is how it makes us feel. Religion is merely a preference, not unlike the choice of a meal or the color of your car. *Time* Magazine recently heralded this all-religions-are-the-same idea with a flag-draped, "subscribe now" ad bearing the banner, "God, Allah, Krishna, Waheguru, Jehovah bless America." Never mind that the names invoked represent monotheists, Trinitarian monotheists, and polytheists. It's all the same, as *Time* sees it.

And because all religions are equally true, any claim to the truth is absolutist and bigoted. Those who insist that they have the truth are divisive and "imperialist"—the equivalent to intellectual fascists[4]—and un-American—even anti-American. Proselytizing is the worst of sins!

The effect of today's intransigent, ironically intolerant pluralism upon evangelical Christianity has been significant. According to James Davidson Hunter's impeccable research in *Evangelicalism: The Coming Generation*, almost 60 percent of students at Christian colleges and seminaries question whether faith in Jesus is actually necessary for salvation.[5] Evangelical Christianity is losing its nerve under the fire of relentless pluralism—and is inventing new theologies to accommodate culture. These are tough days, especially for those in high school and below. Change is coming so fast that the world that awaits young men and women when they finish high school will little resemble what they have known in the past. Given pluralism's trajectory, an unforgiving (even dictatorial) pluralism may be ahead.

One thing is certain: Nothing will set you apart from culture more than the exclusive claims of Christianity. And it is here that we must intentionally set ourselves apart—because if we do not, we will have no message for the world! (For a clear explanation of the Gospel, see Appendix I: "The Gospel—Old and New.")

HEALTHY PLURALISM

What, then, are we to make of pluralism? How are we to understand it? And how are we to respond to it? For starters, *pluralism* is not a dirty word; it describes a beautiful thing. To get the idea, imagine a world without the taste of Mexican cuisine—or Chinese—or French—or Italian—or Thai—or Middle Eastern—or Greek—or German—or Indian—or Polish—or Swedish—or Norwegian. Unthinkable! A world without the aroma of tortillas, or basil and garlic, or curry—unbearable!

These are merely the aromas of pluralism. How enriching they are! But the riches of pluralism go far deeper. Think of the music, the rhythms, the dances, the architectures, the arts, the color palettes, the styles, the literatures, and the customs of all the various cultures. And then there are the people themselves in all their marvelous profiles, features, and pigments. Such extravagant beauty. God created all this and celebrates it now, as he will in the eschaton: "After this I looked, and behold, a great multitude that no one could number, from every nation, from all tribes and peoples and languages, standing before the throne and before the Lamb, clothed in white robes, with palm branches in their hands" (Revelation 7:9).

The purest use of pluralism is *descriptive*: It simply describes diversity. This use has no agenda or viewpoint to promote. It simply describes modern western society. Chicago or New York or Los Angeles is pluralistic.

There also is the virtue of pluralistic tolerance, by which I mean an *attitude* of tolerance. Pluralistic social tolerance calls for love and understanding toward people who think and believe differently than we do. It celebrates and protects their uniqueness. Likewise, legal tolerance calls us to protect others' rights to follow any religion or no religion at all. But such tolerance does not mean that we are to be intellectually tolerant, acting as if another's ideas or beliefs are true simply because people hold them. Pluralistic toleration does not mean that we do not try to convince others that they are wrong.[6]

Pluralism that is healthy is both descriptive and tolerant. It celebrates life and diversity. This is not to say that it does not have its dangers because, as Kennedy Cabinet member and distinguished Harvard historian Arthur Schlesinger warned in his book *The Disuniting of America*, as contentious groups grow in size and demand greater autonomy, refusing the "melting pot," America may prove ungovernable.[7] But that is another issue. Diversity is nevertheless innately beautiful.

UNHEALTHY PLURALISM

Philosophical pluralism. Whereas *descriptive* pluralism describes diversity and practices tolerance, *prescriptive* pluralism demands diversity and tolerance. There is a universe of difference between descriptive and prescriptive pluralism.

Prescriptive pluralism is unhealthy for diversity, even though it demands it. Prescriptive pluralism is a philosophy of tolerance that tolerates no other. It is based on a loose set of attitudes called modernity, which insists that objective truth cannot be known and that all we can do is impose subjective categories on reality. Therefore truth for you is not truth for someone else. So if you say that you have the truth and the truth is for everyone, you're arrogant. Further, you're to be watched carefully. You cannot be good for society because your insistence that you are right and others are wrong is divisive—imperialistic—fascist. As humanist Allan Bloom wrote in *The Closing of the American Mind*:

> The true believer is in the real danger. The study of history and of culture teaches that all the world was mad in the past; men always thought that they were right, and that led to wars, persecutions, slavery, xenophobia, racism and chauvinism. The point is not to correct the mistakes and really be right; rather it is not to think that you are right at all.[8]

This makes Franklin Graham, and people like him, dangerous—troublers of society.

Theological pluralism. Theological pluralism comes out of philosophical pluralism. If truth is relative and determined by the inner self, then all religions are equally true. This position was given widespread publicity at the 1893 World's Parliament of Religions here in Chicago in the Columbian Exposition by Hindu Swami Vivekananda, who proclaimed that he was "proud to belong to a religion that has taught the world both tolerance and universal acceptance. We believe not only in universal toleration, but we accept all religions as true."[9]

The Swami was referencing the *Bhagavad Gita*, which declares, "Howsoever men may approach me, even so do I accept them; for, on all sides, whatsoever path they may choose is mine."[10] Today liberal western theologians like John Hick, of *The Myth of God Incarnate* fame, have taken this as their mantra. This kind of thinking, as it is practiced today in America, demands that you not only rightly make space for a neighbor to believe what he believes, but that you also refrain from publicly disagreeing with him.

Such all-paths-lead-to-God thinking has no root in Christianity, comparative religion, or logic, for the following reasons:

• The various religions of the world do not worship the same universal essence or God, but contradictory concepts of God.

• The religions of the world disagree as to the problem of man, whereas Christianity sees it to be sin against a righteous God. Hinduism and Buddhism view the problem as "rather a profound ignorance, blindness, or confusion regarding the nature of reality."[11]

• All religions have differing concepts and proposals for salvation; to argue that they are really the same is intellectually patronizing.

• The religions of the world do not agree as to what constitutes good conduct (just consider temple prostitution, Aztec human sacrifice, and Hindu widow burning).

Consistent pluralism, if practiced, tolerates the morally intolerable.[12] But the one thing it does not tolerate is the claim that Christ is the truth, or that there is only one way to salvation. Proclaim that on the major networks and declare the corollary that other religions are in error, and you'll be given opportunity to recant. Such hubris we Christians have. Such insensitivity. Such divisiveness. And it is claimed that this is what is "wrong with America."

Christianity's Exclusivism

Nevertheless, the Bible and Christ are radically exclusive. Following the miraculous deliverance of the Exodus, Moses recalled God's works on Israel's behalf and twice declared the exclusivity of their God, saying, "To you it was shown, that you might know that the LORD is God; there is no other besides him" (Deuteronomy 4:35). Again, "Know therefore today, and lay it to your heart, that the LORD is God in heaven above and on the earth beneath; there is no other" (v. 39). Later Isaiah used the same phrase in his famous account of God's sovereignty in history where God himself five times says, "I am the LORD, and there is no other" (45:5-6, 18, 21-22). Clearly, the Bible rules out a smorgasbord of world religions.

John 3:16, the Gospel's most famous text, offers eternal life through Christ alone: "For God so loved the world, that he gave his only Son, that whoever believes in him should not perish but have eternal life. For God did not send his Son into the world to condemn the world, but in order that the world might be saved through him" (John 3:16-17). But note that this lovely offer is linked to the fact that all outside Christ are condemned: "Whoever believes in him is not condemned, but whoever does not believe is condemned already, because he has not believed in the name of the only Son of God" (v. 18). Note also that the chapter closes with this solemn reiteration: "Whoever believes in the Son has eternal life; whoever does not obey the Son shall not see life, but the wrath of God remains on him" (v. 36). John presents Jesus as the only way.

And this is how Jesus personally presents himself. As the Great Shepherd, he said, "Truly, truly, I say to you, I am the door of the sheep. All who came before me are thieves and robbers, but the sheep did not listen to them. I am the door. If anyone enters by me, he will be saved and will go in and out and find pasture" (John 10:7-9). And, of course, we have this radically exclusive statement from his own lips, "I am the way, and the truth, and the life. No one comes to the Father except through me" (John 14:6). However you parse it, it can only mean one thing: There is only one way of salvation. Those who reject it will have to deal with Christ himself.

The apostles believed this with all their hearts. When Peter and John stood before the same Sanhedrin that had condemned Jesus, Peter, quoting messianic lines from Psalm 18, declared of Christ, "This Jesus is the stone that was rejected by you, the builders, which has become the cornerstone. And there is salvation in no one else, for there is no other name under heaven given among men by which we must be saved" (Acts 4:11-12). Peter and John both lived and died, staking their whole lives on this. Paul so believed that all apart from Christ were lost that he said, "I am speaking the truth in Christ—I am not lying; my conscience bears me witness in the Holy Spirit—that I have great sorrow and unceasing anguish in my heart. For I could wish that I myself were accursed and cut off from Christ for the sake of my brothers, my kinsmen according to the flesh" (Romans 9:1-3). His amazing passion rested on the exclusivity of Christ.

Why the exclusivity of Christ? Why is he the only way? The heart of the answer lies in how radically lost and radically sinful we are. This is precisely what the world's religions do not understand and will not embrace. Every religious system apart from Christianity bases "salvation," as it defines it, on works. This is explicitly true in salvation-through-reincarnation systems like Hinduism and Buddhism with its eightfold path to Nirvana. In both, progress upward is conditioned on good works in this life. Aside from the falsity of this doctrine, given the true depth of human sin, the only possible reincarnation for humans would be a downward spiral.

And Islam? Contrary to biblical revelation, Islam believes that people are born good, and that life is a walk on a sword's edge. The walk is maintained by not falling into sin. And if one does not fall from the razor's walk, perhaps Allah will grant paradise in the end.

But the Bible knows no such bootstrap salvation because it is impossible. We are simply too sinful and too lost. Paul's litany of human depravity in Romans 3:9-18 declares that all humanity is profoundly sinful in soul, speech, and actions: "None is righteous, no, not one" (v. 10). Even the ostensible seeking of world religions is not a seeking after the true God: "no one understands; no one seeks for God" (v. 10). The truth, as Paul states in Ephesians 2:1, is that all are dead in their transgressions and sins. The spiritually dead can do nothing to merit salvation. This is biblical reality. This is what the apostolic church believed. This is what biblical orthodoxy has always held.

This is why there is no salvation apart from Christ's atoning work on the cross. It was and is the only way. Remember Christ's prayer in Gethsemane? "Father, if you are willing, remove this cup from me. Nevertheless, not my will, but yours, be done" (Luke 22:42). Though in the Upper Room he had declared, "This cup that is poured out for you is the new covenant in my blood" (22:20), thus embracing his death on the cross, he now recoiled at the personal horror he was about to endure. The cup was so awful, so unbearable, so appalling, so horrendous that Jesus' soul revulsed and convulsed. How could he drink such filth? How could he bear his Father's wrath?

"Father, if there is any possible way out, please do it—yet not my will, but yours be done." It was a real prayer from the incarnate God-man. Oh, that there was another way! Jesus was caught between two proper desires. It is proper to want to avoid death, alienation, and wrath. It is also proper and best to want to do God's will, whatever the cost. Jesus chose the best! "Your will be done!" was the cry of the conqueror. Jesus wanted the Father's will more than anything else.

There in the garden the perfect, omnipotent Father listened to his perfect Son's agonized pleading for an alternative way. And if there was any other way he would have done it. But since there was not, he willed his Son's death. What a slur to say that God does not care about us! What a blasphemous affront to God to think that sin does not matter! What an outrage to imagine that we are good enough for God to accept us! What a cosmic affront to hold that there is any way apart from Jesus! John's Gospel says it all: "For God so loved the world, that he gave his only Son, that whoever believes in him should not perish but have eternal life" (3:16).

The following passages, all from the lips of the one who drank the cup, constitute the Christian's charge:

> "Go therefore and make disciples of all nations, baptizing them in the name of the Father and of the Son and of the Holy Spirit, teaching them to observe all that I have commanded you. And behold, I am with you always, to the end of the age."
>
> —MATTHEW 28:19-20

> "Thus it is written, that the Christ should suffer and on the third day rise from the dead, and that repentance and forgiveness of sins should be proclaimed in his name to all nations, beginning from Jerusalem. You are witnesses of these things."
>
> —LUKE 24:46-48

"Peace be with you. As the Father has sent me, even so I am sending you."

—JOHN 20:21

"But you will receive power when the Holy Spirit has come upon you, and you will be my witnesses in Jerusalem and in all Judea and Samaria, and to the end of the earth."

—ACTS 1:8

Certainly we must be pluralistic in the authentic sense. We must celebrate diversity. We must be tolerant and civil to those with whom we disagree. Our hearts, our words, our tone must be truly loving.

But we must not be cowed by the politically correct, relativist, intolerant "pluralism" of our day, which insists that truth is relative—that all religions are equally true and valid—that you must not only leave room for your neighbor to believe what he wants, but that you must refrain from saying that he is wrong.

As the church, we must set ourselves apart from the lockstep pluralism of our day and declare that Jesus is *the* way, *the* truth, and *the* life, and that no one comes to the Father but through him. And we must declare, when called to do so, that all other roads are false.

It has been true, and always will be, that a church that truly believes the Gospel is a church that will win the lost for Christ!

FOR REFLECTION AND APPLICATION

• What examples of pluralism have you seen in Christian or secular contexts?

• How would healthy pluralism differ from unhealthy pluralism in relation to a neighbor from a different faith?

• Why do even Christians in America tend toward unhealthy pluralism?

• How has pluralism affected your witness to the Gospel?

• Why is the exclusivity of Jesus Christ as the only way of salvation essential?

NOTES

1. Julia Lieblich, "Audience of Many Faiths Joins Schuller in Mosque for an 'Evening of Hope,'" *Chicago Tribune*, November 2, 2001. www.chicagotribune.com/news/local/chicago/ chi011102013nov02.story.

2. Richard N. Ostling, AP religion writer, "Graham the Son Cut from Different Cloth."

3. Franklin Graham, "My View of Islam," *The Wall Street Journal*, December 3, 2001.

4. Alister E. McGrath, *Understanding and Responding to Moral Pluralism* (Wheaton, IL: CACE (Center for Applied Christian Ethics), n.d.), p. 3.

5. James Davidson Hunter, *Evangelicalism: The Coming Generation* (Chicago: The University of Chicago Press, 1987), p. 36.

6. Daniel B. Clendenin, "The Only Way," *Christianity Today*, January 12, 1998. www.christianitytoday.com/ct/8t1034.html.

7. Arthur Schlesinger, *The Disuniting of America* (New York: W. W. Norton & Co., 1991), pp. 117-118.

8. Allan Bloom, *The Closing of the American Mind* (New York: Simon & Schuster, 1987), pp. 25-26.

9. Clendenin, "The Only Way," p. 8.

10. Ibid., p. 9.

11. Ibid., p. 10.

12. Ibid., p. 12.

Set Apart to Save: Marriage

Now when Jesus had finished these sayings, he went away from Galilee and entered the region of Judea beyond the Jordan. And large crowds followed him, and he healed them there. And Pharisees came up to him and tested him by asking, "Is it lawful to divorce one's wife for any cause?" He answered, "Have you not read that he who created them from the beginning made them male and female, and said, 'Therefore a man shall leave his father and his mother and hold fast to his wife, and they shall become one flesh'? So they are no longer two but one flesh. What therefore God has joined together, let not man separate." They said to him, "Why then did Moses command one to give a certificate of divorce and to send her away?" He said to them, "Because of your hardness of heart Moses allowed you to divorce your wives, but from the beginning it was not so. And I say to you: whoever divorces his wife, except for sexual immorality, and marries another, commits adultery." The disciples said to him, "If such is the case of a man with his wife, it is better not to marry." But he said to them, "Not everyone can receive this saying, but only those to whom it is given."

MATTHEW 19:1-11

The protection and perpetuation of marriage is a difficult and painful topic, for several reasons. Virtually everyone has been touched by the dissolution of the marriage of someone they love. Divorce is very close to home for all of us—tragically close. Also, many of you have experienced divorce. Some of you bear the guilt for what happened. Hopefully you've repented. Others are simply victims. You're certainly not perfect, but the truth is, you don't bear an ounce of responsibility for what happened. Some are in the midst of the extended misery of dissolution right now. The nightmare you're experiencing was never anticipated. You wish that you could wake up and find it is only a bad dream.

In tackling the subject of divorce, my intention is first and foremost scriptural and pastoral in tone and application. My purpose is to elevate and preserve marriage. But wherever you are, whatever your history, whether you bear some guilt or not, or whether you are a victim or a child of divorced parents, the power of God to work through the situation is not limited. As you look to him, you can expect him to work *redemptively* in your life. There always is more grace. And as you look to him you can expect his blessings.

Citizen magazine carried a cover story entitled "Divorce: Bible-Belt Style." The author, Glenn Stanton, made penetrating observations about the divorce and remarriage of a Christian megastar. Stanton wrote:

> She said she recognized that God hates divorce, but she also realized a more personal and freeing truth. In August 1998, after undergoing what she called "tons of marital counseling," she went to the pastors with whom she had sought guidance and to her then-husband . . . and told them all, "I believe and trust that I've been released from this [marriage]. And I say that knowing that even the Bible says the heart is deceitful."
>
> She further explained how she knew this was God's will, and "to the best of my level of peace, I had a very settled, unshakable feeling about the path that I was going to follow."
>
> Some advice from another counselor added to her blessed assurance. . . . "He said, '. . . God made marriage for people. He didn't make people for marriage. . . . He provided this so that people could enjoy each other to the fullest. I say if you have two people that are not thriving healthily in a situation, I say remove the marriage.'"[1]

Those were hollow chords from the megastar as she appealed to the imperium of her own feelings and pleasure—her "unshakable feeling" that she was released from her marriage, plus the necessity that in marriage "people . . . enjoy each other to the fullest." I wonder how these lyrics played with the Jesus she sings about. The singer pursued a typical pro forma divorce and married a country singer in an outdoor service near Nashville with an intimate gathering of friends and family.

It may seem ironic that the Bible-toting pop star's remarks and divorce and remarriage took place on the very buckle of the so-called Bible Belt. But it is not. Recent evidence from demographers indicates that no region of the nation has a higher divorce rate than the Bible Belt (Tennessee, Arkansas, Alabama, and Oklahoma). Says Stanton, "The American Southeast is loaded with churches, and flush with conservative values, but for some reason, overflowing with divorce. At the news [of the pop star's divorce], the left-leaning, online magazine *Salon* took delight in sarcastically quipping that the Bible Belt is 'where families pray together, but apparently can't stay together.'"[2]

BIBLE BELT DIVORCE

Here are the most up-to-date facts. Nationally 25 percent of all adults have experienced at least one divorce during their lifetime (one out of four). This 25 percent statistic breaks down between born-again and non-born-again people like this: 24 percent of non-born-again people have suffered divorce, while 27 percent of born-again Christians have been divorced. Born-again Christians are more likely to go through a marital split than are non-Christians.[3] George Barna notes:

> Surprisingly, the Christian denomination whose adherents have the highest likelihood of getting divorced are Baptists. Nationally, 29% of all Baptist adults have been divorced. The only Christian group to surpass that level are those associated with non-denominational Protestant churches: 34% of those adults have undergone a divorce. Of the nation's major Christian groups, Catholics and Lutherans have the lowest percentage of divorced individuals (21%).[4]

Embarrassingly, self-designated atheists and agnostics are well below the born-again norm at 21 percent.[5] The facts are irrefutable: The Bible Belt's Baptist and non-denominational churches (at 29 and 35 percent respectively) far outstrip general culture's 25 percent divorce rate and the 21 percent of atheists and agnostics. At last conservative Christians are out in front leading culture—in divorce!

Notwithstanding some question about how many of the respondents were born-again at the time of their divorce, or about the accuracy of the self-designation born-again, or the fact that many non-Christians cohabit instead of marry, all the indicators are that at best the divorce rate of Christians is the same as general culture, and at the worst scandalously higher. And further, the so-called Bible Belt leads the way. According to the Associated Press, "No state has been more embarrassed by the divorce problem than Oklahoma. Over the past few months, Gov. Frank Keating has enlisted clergymen, academics, lawyers and psychologists in a campaign to reduce the divorce rate by a third within 10 years. In neighboring Arkansas, state officials hope to halve the divorce rate by 2010."[6]

WHY THE BUCKLE'S STATS?

Why are the Bible Belt's statistics so high when compared to the Northeast, where only 19 percent of the residents have been divorced? Certainly there are social factors in that people marry earlier in the South and have lower incomes. But even more telling is the fact that the Northeast has large populations of Catholics and Lutherans, both of which have the lowest divorce rates of all Christian denominations. And significantly, both have theologies that are less tolerant of divorce than the conservative denominations that characterize the South.[7]

What, then, is it about the belief systems in conservative southern churches that makes them (and born-again Christians in general) more open to divorce? The answer is in three big words: antinomianism, narcissism, and hedonism. These words may sound difficult, but the ideas they represent are simple.

Antinomianism. Antinomianism comes from the Greek words *anti* (against) and *nomos* (law) and signifies opposition to the law. It insists that the moral law is not binding on Christians as a rule of life. Antinomianism describes people who ignore any law apart from their own subjective opinions—opinions that they characteristically attribute to the Holy Spirit.[8] Scriptural support for this is quoted out of context: "But if you are led by the Spirit, you are not under the law" (Galatians 5:18). When the supposed leading of the Holy Spirit conflicts with God's law, the alleged guidance of the Spirit, it is thought, supersedes God's law.[9] The rhetoric of antinomianism is, "We're not under the law, but grace. We've been set free from the law."

Those who insist that Scripture and Christ himself lay down immutable laws are called "legalists." Antinomians insist that we have been saved from the law, and that where the Spirit is, there is freedom. Phrases like "I believe and trust that I've been set free from this [marriage]" characterize this kind of thinking.

Narcissism. Narcissism is, of course, self-love. Today's world is marked by a self-interest and ego-centeredness that increasingly reduces all relationships to the question, "What am I getting out of it?" This retreat into self has become a fact of evangelical life. As James Davidson Hunter wrote in his landmark *Evangelicals: The Coming Generation*: "The fascination with the self and with human subjectivity has become a well-established cultural feature of evangelicalism in the latter part of the twentieth century, not an ephemeral fashion among the younger generation."[10] Self-focus diminishes God-focus, so that God is increasingly relegated to the periphery of life, leaving us open to other invasions of worldliness.

Perhaps if a statue of the modern narcissistic world were sculpted, it would be an androgynous figure with its arms wrapped around itself kissing its mirror image. Narcissism shrinks the soul and reduces all relations to the question of self—an attitude that is cyanide to marriage.

Hedonism. Hedonism is the pursuit of pleasure. As we noted earlier, in George Orwell's *1984* people are controlled by inflicting pain, whereas in Aldous Huxley's *Brave New World* they are controlled by inflicting pleasure. Here in the West, Huxley's vision is reality, for we allow our pleasures to control us. For many Christians, marriage has become a provisional relationship, conditional on enjoyment. For them, the arbiter of moral questions has become the secular therapist rather than God's Word. Recall the therapist's advice: "God made marriage for people. He didn't make people for marriage. . . . He provided this so people could enjoy each other to the fullest. I say if you have two people that are not thriving healthily in a situation, I say remove the marriage." In other words, "Do it! We're under grace. Christianity is for us, and our happiness is the highest good." Now here's a theology we can live with—any way we want.

Listen to this "great" advice from *Divorce: How and When to Let Go*: "Letting go of your marriage—if it is no longer fulfilling—can be the most successful thing you've ever done. Getting a divorce can be a positive, problem-solving growth-oriented step. It can be a personal triumph."[11] Amazing! By making self-fulfillment the guiding principle of life, you can call failure success, disintegration growth, and disaster triumph.

What the Bible Says

But this is not what the Bible says. In fact, earliest revelation reveals that immediately after recording Adam's joyous cry at his first sight of Eve, Moses added this comment: "Therefore a man shall leave his father and his mother and hold fast to his wife, and they shall become one flesh" (Genesis 2:24). Moses understood that the marriage involves leaving and cleaving in permanent, profound intimacy.

And that is how Christ himself understood it when he was asked by the Pharisees about divorce: "He answered, 'Have you not read that he who created them from the beginning made them male and female, and said, "Therefore a man shall leave his father and his mother and hold fast to his wife, and they shall become one flesh"? So they are no longer two but one flesh. What therefore God has joined together, let not man separate'" (Matthew 19:4-6). So there we have it. It is dominical—from the lips of the Lord himself. In the beginning divorce was inconceivable and impossible. There was no hint of divorce. God's ideal was, and is, monogamous, intimate, enduring marriage. Anything less is a departure from the divine model.

The Pharisees had alluded to an ancient controversy in Deuteronomy 24 by asking if a man may divorce his wife for any reason at all. Jesus had responded by saying that divorce is not God's standard. Thus the Pharisees countered with another reference to Deuteronomy 24, as we read in verse 7: "Why then did Moses command one to give a certificate of divorce and to send her away?" Their argument was, "Moses made provision for divorce in Deuteronomy 24:1. How, then, can you say it is not part of the ideal?"

Note Jesus' answer in verse 8: "Because of your hardness of heart Moses allowed you to divorce your wives, but from the beginning it was not so." His answer corrected the Pharisees, because Moses only *permitted* divorce. He didn't *command* it, as the Pharisees asserted. What Moses *did* command was the granting of a divorce certificate for the woman's protection. Without a certificate she would be subject to exploitation and even recrimination.

The reason God allowed divorce was that the hearts of the men of Israel were "hard." This was a divine concession to human weakness, a concession to man's sinfulness, but it cannot be taken as approval. It was reluctant permission at best.

The exception. Understanding this, we come to the very center of Christ's teaching as to why and when divorce is permitted: "And I say to you: whoever divorces his wife, *except for sexual immorality*, and marries another, commits adultery" (v. 9, emphasis mine). Here the meaning rests upon the correct interpretation of the phrase "except for sexual immorality," and especially the simple word "immorality" (other translations: "unfaithfulness"). The Greek word here is *porneia*, from which we derive the English word *pornography*. Greek dictionaries tell us that *porneia* means unchastity, fornication, prostitution, or other kinds of unlawful intercourse. When *porneia* is applied to married persons, it means, as our text says, sexual immorality, marital unfaithfulness, illicit intercourse, which may involve adultery, homosexuality, bestiality, and the like.

We must note (and this is very important) that all these offenses were originally punished by death under Mosaic Law. These sins terminated marriage not by divorce but by death! However, by Jesus' time the Roman occupation and its legal system had made the death sentence for such offenses difficult to obtain. Jewish practice had therefore *substituted divorce for death*. This is why the rabbinical schools of Hillel and Shammai were not discussing whether divorce is permissible for adultery. Divorce was a given, not only for adultery, but for many lesser offenses. The point is that Jesus was far stricter than the rabbinical disputants because he superseded the teaching of Deuteronomy 24 and said that the only grounds by which one could divorce his or her spouse was marital unfaithfulness, an offense that was originally punished by death.

The simple, plain meaning of Jesus' words in Matthew 19:9 ("And I say to you: whoever divorces his wife, except for sexual immorality, and marries another, commits adultery") is that divorce is allowed if your mate is guilty of marital unfaithfulness. If you divorce for any other reason and remarry, it is you who commits adultery. This is likewise the meaning of Jesus' similar statement in the Sermon on the Mount in Matthew 5:32—"But I say to you that everyone who divorces his wife, except on the ground of sexual immorality, makes her commit adultery. And whoever marries a divorced woman commits adultery." Jesus' teaching is plain to see. The Lord Jesus Christ permitted divorce and remarriage on one ground, and one ground only: marital unfaithfulness.

Notice that he permitted it—he did not command it. Divorce is never mandatory. Too often men and women eagerly pounce on the infidelity of their mate as the opportunity to get out of a relationship they haven't liked anyway. It's so easy to look for a way out instead of working through the problems. We should not regard a one-time affair as an easy excuse for divorce. Rather, we should think about this issue in terms of an unfaithful lifestyle—a mate who refuses to turn from his or her adulterous ways.

Jesus' exception should be viewed like this: No matter how rough things are, regardless of the stress and strain or whatever is said about compatibility and temperament, nothing allows for divorce except one thing—*unfaithfulness*. And then it is not to be used as an excuse to get out of the marriage.

Jesus had done away completely with the loopholes of the Mosaic divorce provision (Deuteronomy 24:1). This was revolutionary. The disciples' response indicates just how radical Jesus' teaching was: "If such is the case of a man with his wife, it is better not to marry" (Matthew 19:10). They were shocked by the radical permanence of marriage. If the only ground for divorce was unfaithfulness, if none of the exceptions suggested by Hillel and Shammai were valid, it was better to stay single! So much then for our culture's provisional antinomian, narcissistic, hedonistic approach to marriage. If that is the way you think, it is better not to marry.

And here it must be said that if we hope to reach the world, the church must become a culture in which divorce is an aberration. Divorce happens—because of sin. There is no way to "divorce-proof" your marriage, as some books suggest. Some of the godliest people you will ever meet are its victims.

So it is not to those that I say this. But Christian divorce *lies* about Christ and the church. Christ and his bride will never be separated. Christ loved the church as his own body and gave himself for her. His marriage to the church is eternal. And this is what the world needs to see in our relationships. How can we have a message to the world when we lead the way in divorce?

WHAT WE MUST DO

I regularly have the best view at Christian weddings as I stand about three feet from the joyous couple. The skin of the couple glows amber from the flickering candles behind me. I see everything: the moist eyes, the trembling hands, the surreptitious wink, the mutual earnestness of soul. I hear the words their parents said before them: ". . . for better, for worse; for richer, for poorer; in sickness and in health . . ." They are submitting to the larger logics of life, to the solidarity of the Christian community, to "otherness," to life itself.

Sometimes in my enjoyment I let it all blur for a moment and imagine the ultimate wedding where Christ will officially take us to himself, and then I blink back to the living parable before me. How will the couple fare over the years? Will she reverence her husband? Will he love his beautiful bride as Christ loved the church and gave himself for her? Will he love her with an elevating, sanctifying love? Will he love her as he loves himself? I pray it will be so.

Wedding days are such joy. I love the celebration. I love the family and church gathered in solidarity. I love the sentiment and the wine of joy flowing freely.

The cross. At the same time, I know that without the cross it is not a Christian marriage. Marriage is about dying because that is what Jesus did for his bride. At marriage a single man and a single woman die to self, and the two become one flesh. The wedding marks the end of the former man and woman.

But the wedding is only the beginning of death.[12] Recognizing this, Mike Mason, author of the classic *The Mystery of Marriage*, says pointedly that marital love is like death—it wants all of us. If you do not understand this, you do not know what marital love is. It claims everything. And then as Mason reaches for a metaphor to make this point, he likens marital love to a man-eating shark! "And who has not been frightened almost to death by love's dark shadow gliding swift and huge as an interstellar shark, like a swimming mountain, through the deepest waters of our being, through depths we never knew we had?"[13] The realization of what this call means may first be frightening, but it is beautiful. Christian marriage vows are the inception of a lifelong practice of death, of giving over not all you *have*, but all you *are*.

The blood-drenched cross needs to be lifted high at a Christian wedding because that is what makes it Christian. But of course, the cross is also the road to a particular joy—"For whoever would save his life will lose it, but whoever loses his life for my sake will find it" (Matthew 16:25).

The covenant. Today one of the most popular seminars in our nation is on how to write prenuptial agreements. The covenantal significance of marriage is simply passé. Instead of being viewed as a lifelong commitment sealed with an oath before God, marriage has become a contractual agreement that is dissolvable any time—at will.

But Christian marriage is a covenantal relationship to death, not a contract. It cannot be Christian if it is contractual or conditional. Christian marriage calls for a solemn oath to God, a couple's swearing to God that they will never break their covenant. Because of this, I ask every couple who asks me to do their wedding ceremony that if they discover after marriage that the other is not what the spouse expected, or due to accident or sickness or dementia undergoes radical change and becomes radically altered—if this happens, do they imagine that there is a way out? Because if they do, I cannot conduct the ceremony. And then at the wedding, before they repeat their nuptial vows, I say, "These vows are for life. They are never ever to be broken. God and this congregation and your family are witnesses."

Marriage that rests on an oath of covenant enjoys two substantial benefits. First, it provides security and freedom. Lifetime commitment, in which divorce is out of the question, gives space to work things out. There is no threat that if problems aren't solved immediately, the marriage is in danger. Divorce is not a part of the marital vocabulary, even in the most heated disagreements. The threat is nonexistent and never made. A mutual covenant then means that we have a lifetime to bond and explore our oneness.[14]

Second, the marriage covenant challenges us to grow in our marriages. Since the commitment is for life, it is to our mutual benefit to grow in all aspects of marriage. This encourages husbands and wives to know each other. Commitment enhances mutual growth. A mutual covenantal oath provides the foundation for the architecture of a beautiful life together.

Christ. There is the cross, there is the covenant, and of course there is Christ. This is the grand key to marriage. As Christians, we are already married to him. And thus when Christ the bridegroom is

the center of our marriage, he graces our marital love. Temple
Gardner caught it perfectly with this prayer:

> *That I may come near to her, draw*
> *me nearer to Thee than to her,*
> > *make me know Thee more than her,*
>
> *That I may love her with a perfect*
> *love . . .*
> > *cause me to love Thee more than her.*

The cross—our willing death. The covenant—our sacred word.
Christ—our Savior and Lord. These are the elements of a marriage
that lasts.

And the importance of an enduring marriage extends far beyond
us. If we hope to reach the world, the church must become a culture
in which divorce is an aberration. The faithfulness of Christ to his
church must be seen in our faithfulness to one another. The love of
Christ for his church must be seen in the way we love one another.

We must say no to antinomianism that ignores God's commands
in order to follow feelings, and no to narcissism, the cyanide of self-
love, and no to hedonism, the reign of pleasure. And then we must
say yes to the cross and the covenant and Christ—for his glory in the
church and among the nations.

To Christian couples, I would suggest that you take some time
alone and reaffirm your love to each other and reaffirm your commitment.

The cross. Reaffirm that the cross is the center of your marriage,
and that you will joyfully die for each other.

The covenant. Reaffirm that your marriage covenant is for life, and
that you will never ever break it.

Christ. Reaffirm that you are both "in Christ" the bridegroom,
and pray that you will love him more than each other.

And to those considering marriage, you must first embrace the
cross and the covenant and Christ if you are to have a Christian
marriage.

FOR REFLECTION AND APPLICATION

• Why do you think the divorce rate among Christians is generally higher than the divorce rate among non-Christians?

• What are the likely reactions to Jesus' teaching that marital unfaithfulness is the only allowable basis for divorce and remarriage? How would you respond to these reactions?

• How should the cross of Christ, the covenant marriage vows, and the centrality of Christ affect our attitudes and behaviors in marriage?

NOTES

1. Glenn T. Stanton, "Divorce: Bible-Belt Style," *Citizen* magazine (Focus on the Family, 2000). www.family.org/cforum/citizenmag/coverstory/a11624.html.

2. Ibid.

3. Barna Research On Line, "Christians Are More Likely to Experience Divorce Than Are Non-Christians," December 21, 1999. www.barna.org/cgi/PagePressRelease.asp?PressReleaseID=39% Reference=C

4. Ibid.

5. Ibid.

6. David Crary, "Bible Belt Leads U.S. in Divorces," Associated Press, November 12, 1999. www.nepa.org/pd/social/pd111999g.html.

7. Stanton, "Divorce: Bible-Belt Style," p. 5.

8. Everett F. Harrison, ed., *Baker's Dictionary of Theology* (Grand Rapids, MI: Baker, 1973), p. 48.

9. Stanton, "Divorce: Bible-Belt Style," p. 5.

10. James Davidson Hunter, *Evangelicalism: The Coming Generation* (Chicago: University of Chicago Press, 1987), p. 69.

11. John R. W. Stott, *Issues Facing Christians Today* (London: Marshall, Morgan & Scott, 1984), p. 260.

12. Peter J. Leithart, "When Marriage Is Dying," *Touchstone*, December 2001, p. 20.

13. Mike Mason, *The Mystery of Marriage* (Portland: Multnomah, 1985), p. 52.

14. Gloria Gaither, Gigi Graham Tchividjian, Susan Alexander Yates, *Marriage: Questions Women Ask* (Portland: Multnomah, 1992), p. 68.

10

Set Apart to Save:
Church and the Lord's Day

"Remember the Sabbath day, to keep it holy. Six days you shall labor, and do all your work, but the seventh day is a Sabbath to the LORD your God. On it you shall not do any work, you, or your son, or your daughter, your male servant, or your female servant, or your livestock, or the sojourner who is within your gates. For in six days the LORD made heaven and earth, the sea, and all that is in them, and rested the seventh day. Therefore the LORD blessed the Sabbath day and made it holy." . . . But on the first day of the week, at early dawn, they went to the tomb, taking the spices they had prepared. And they found the stone rolled away from the tomb, but when they went in they did not find the body of the Lord Jesus.

—EXODUS 20:8-11; LUKE 24:1-3

When viewed in terms of numbers, American evangelicalism would seem to be thriving. This impression of vitality is made especially visible by the rise of mega-churches whose individual memberships number in the thousands.

But when examined in light of the actual superficiality of church commitment and understanding of the Gospel, the numbers are highly misleading. Given the magnitude of what the Bible declares the church to be and what it has historically meant, it is ironic that such scant allegiance is given to the church today. Pollster George Barna notes that "the average adult thinks that belonging to a church is good for other people, but represents unnecessary bondage and baggage for himself."[1] Today there are droves of professing

Christians who have never been committed to the local expression of Christ's body, and never intend to be.

WELCOME TO THE UNCOMMITTED

At least six trends that are common on the landscape of contemporary American Christianity severely mar the picture of what appears to be a flourishing Christian church. When compared to these trends, the attendance figures are mere window dressing. Here are the trends that tell the hidden story:

Hitchhiker Christians. Evangelicalism is blanketed with a malaise of conditional loyalty that has produced an army of church hitchhikers. The hitchhiker's thumb says, "You buy the car, pay for repairs and upkeep and insurance, fill the car with gas—and I'll ride with you. But if you have an accident, you are on your own! And I'll probably sue." So it is with the credo of many of today's church attenders: "You go to the meetings and serve on the boards and committees, you grapple with the issues and do the work of the church and pay the bills—and I'll come along for the ride. But if things do not suit me, I'll criticize and complain and probably bail out. My thumb is always out for a better ride."

Today, at the beginning of the third millennium, we have a phenomenon unthinkable in any other century: churchless Christians. Many professed Christians are nomadic hitchhikers without accountability, without discipline, without discipleship, living apart from the regular benefits of the ordinances, and, perhaps most revealing, without responsibility. If you don't join, you don't have to attend, serve, or give. You can be on the perpetual "take." And it never costs! If your family is being served by, say, three churches, who will ever know where your money goes? Consumerism without paying—that's the ultimate. Actually, there is a price that will be paid, and the price may be higher than ever dreamed.

The consumer mentality. The provisional loyalty I have noted is fueled by a consumer ethos that picks and chooses here and there to fill an ecclesiastical shopping list. Ecclesiastical shoppers attend one church for the preaching, send their children to a second church for its youth program, and go to a third church's small group. Their motto is to ask, "What's in it for me?" In my experience, this attitude runs especially strong in people who were raised after the entitlement movement set in (the so-called Generation X). Entitlement has encouraged those who have been influenced by it to think naturally in terms of receiving rather than contributing.

Spectator Christianity. There have always been some who hang at the church's fringes as spectators. But until now it has not been considered normal or acceptable, much less encouraged. Spectator Christianity feeds on the delusion that virtue can come through viewing, much like the football fan who imagines that he ingests strength and daring while watching his favorite pro team. Spectator sports and spectator Christianity produce the same thing—fans who cheer the players on while they themselves are in desperate need of engagement and meaning.

Drive-through Christians. The nice thing about drive-through restaurants is that you can get what you want in a minimum of time with no more effort than a turn of your power steering. The tragic result is a drive-through nation of overweight, unfit people with an addiction to fast foods. So it is with drive-through Christians, who get their "church fix" out of the way by attending a weeknight church service or the early service on Sunday morning so the family can save the bulk of Sunday for the all-important soccer game or recreational trip. Of course, there is an unhappy price extracted over time in the habits and the arteries of a flabby soul—a family that is unfit for the battles of life and has no conception of being Christian soldiers in the great spiritual battle.

Relationless Christianity. The Bible pictures Christians as people who live in relationship to Christ and to one another by virtue of their being members of Christ's body, the church. Indeed, Jesus' Upper-Room prayer taught that the quality of Christian relationships is an essential aspect of the church's witness to the world: "I in them and you in me, that they may become perfectly one, so that the world may know that you sent me . . ." (John 17:23). How ironic, then, that there are actually churches that trade in anonymity, going so far as to abolish membership and the registry of guests. Some churches have even replaced a pastor-in-the-flesh for a video-projected preacher on the screen—a "virtual reality" version of the church. For some, relationless Christianity (is it Christianity?) has become *de jure*. The best church is the one that knows you least and demands the least, it is thought. Of course, the apotheosis is the electronic church where Christ's body can be surveyed by the candid camera and the Word can be heard without responsibility or accountability.

Churchless "worshipers." The current myth is that a life of worship is possible, even better, apart from the church. As one person blithely expressed it, "For 'church,' I go to the mall to my favorite coffee place and spend my morning with the Lord. That is how I worship." This is an updated suburban and yuppie version of how to spend Sunday, changed from its rustic forebear (as expressed by poet Emily Dickinson over a century ago):

> *Some keep the Sabbath going to Church—*
> *I keep it staying at Home—*
> *With a Bobolink for a Chorister—*
> *And an Orchard for a Dome.*

The loss of commitment to the church has naturally produced a casual observance of Sunday as the Lord's day. What in the Old Testament is called a holy day has become for many Christians a holiday. Some seeker-friendly churches schedule their main worship service—the service designed for believing Christians—on Saturday evenings so their parishioners can spend Sundays just like the unbelieving world. Gone is any witness value of a family's going to church on Sunday morning and evening, thereby standing as a lighthouse for Christ in their neighborhoods.

CAUSES OF DE-CHURCHING

Why has the church fallen to such tenuous commitment? There are several reasons. For one, the emphasis of some Christian teachers upon the church's being the "invisible" body of Christ has produced an implicit disregard for the visible church. The promotion of the invisible church idea came from the fact that visible church membership does not mean a person is a Christian, and that it is what is within, unseen in the heart, that counts. Well, yes—except that the inward work of Christ must produce a visible effect and visible commitments. In fact, the lack of visible devotion and commitment may well mean that a person is not a Christian at all. The doctrine of the invisible church is after all unbiblical.

Another reason for the de-churching of many Christians is the historic individualism of evangelical Christianity and the grass-roots American impulse against authority. The natural inclination is to think that you need only an individual relationship with Christ and no other authority. Such thinking produces Christian Lone Rangers who demonstrate their authenticity by riding not to church but out to the badlands, reference Bible in hand, to do battle singlehandedly with the world. Mix theological "invisibleness" with individualism and then with consumerism, and you have the formula for church-hopping nomads. Here consumerism can take on a moral force of its own: It's your responsibility to be a "good shopper" and pay as little as possible for what you get. Consumer loyalty is for the weak-minded, it is claimed; church loyalty is for the lethargic.

THE ANTIDOTE

The first step toward a cure for the ailments I have noted is to recover a biblical vision of what the church truly is. People settle for the anemia I have described because they do not properly understand and value the church. For a short course on the subject, there is no better passage than Hebrews 12:22-24:

> *But you have come to Mount Zion and to the city of the living God, the heavenly Jerusalem, and to innumerable angels in festal gathering, and to the assembly of the firstborn who are enrolled in heaven, and to God, the judge of all, and to the spirits of the righteous made perfect,*

and to Jesus, the mediator of a new covenant, and to the sprinkled blood
that speaks a better word than the blood of Abel.

Every descriptor in this marvelous passage is aglow with realities that
should revolutionize contemporary complacency about the church.

First, we come to the *city of God*: "But you have come to Mount
Zion and to the city of the living God, the heavenly Jerusalem."
Mount Zion was the location of the stronghold that David captured
and made the religious center of his kingdom by bringing to it the
golden Ark of God's presence. When Solomon built the temple and
installed the Ark, Zion/Jerusalem became synonymous with the
earthly dwelling-place of God. In the church we have come to its
heavenly counterpart, the spiritual Jerusalem from above. In one
sense the city is still to come, but at the same time we have already
arrived there in Christ. Christians are now citizens of the heavenly
city and enjoy its privileges (cf. Ephesians 2:6, 19; Philippians 3:20).

Second, as the Church we meet *angels*: "You have come to . . .
innumerable angels in festal gathering." Moses tells us that "ten
thousands of holy ones" attended the giving of the Law
(Deuteronomy 33:2), and from Daniel we hear that "a thousand
thousands served him, and ten thousand times ten thousand stood
before him" (Daniel 7:10). David said, "The chariots of God are twice
ten thousand, thousands upon thousands" (Psalm 68:17).

In the church we come to these dizzying thousands of angels, all
of whom are in joyful celebration. Recently I was with Wheaton
College president Duane Litfin, who at one point waxed expansively
about the wonders of corporate worship and about how the angels
join us in worship. As a result, he said, we need to awaken to this
stunning reality when we gather as a church. He recalled that this was
the awareness of the church in its early centuries. Angels are everywhere—mighty flaming spirits, "ministering spirits sent out to serve
for the sake of those who are to inherit salvation" (Hebrews 1:14),
passing in and out of our lives, moving around us and over us, just as
they did to Jacob of old. In the third century Origen observed, "I do
not doubt that angels are even present in our assembly"; there is "a

double church present, one of men, the other of angels."[2] Poet-preacher George Herbert advised believers to observe Sunday carefully and "think when the bells do chime, 'Tis angel's music; therefore come not late" ("The Church-Porch," stanza 65).

Third, when we are in the church we come to *coheirs*: "to the assembly of the firstborn who are enrolled in heaven." Jesus was the firstborn son *par excellence* and the heir of everything in heaven and earth (cf. Colossians 1:15-20). And by virtue of our union with Christ, we are all "firstborn." All the rights of inheritance go to the firstborn—to us as "fellow heirs with Christ" (Romans 8:17). In the church we do more than come into each other's presence—we come to the fellowship of the eternally rich, firstborn heirs. All of us are rich beyond the dreams of Croesus, and always will be. There are no second- or third-born believers. All are firstborn.

Fourth, we come to *God*: "to God, the judge of all." We come in awe because he is the Judge, but we do not come in utter dread, because his Son has borne the judgment for us. We embrace the Scripture's call, "Let us then with confidence draw near to the throne of grace, that we may receive mercy and find grace to help in time of need" (Hebrews 4:16). This is our highest delight—to gather before our God!

Fifth, we come to the heavenly *Church Triumphant*: "to the spirits of the righteous made perfect." The triumphant are those who have died and gone to heaven. Though they are in heaven and we are on earth, we share a solidarity with those who have gone before. The same spiritual life courses through us as flows through them right now. We share the same secrets and joys as Abraham and Moses and David and Paul and Peter.

Sixth, we come to *Jesus*: "to Jesus, the mediator of a new covenant." At the last supper, Jesus took the cup in his hand and said, "This cup that is poured out for you is the new covenant in my blood" (Luke 22:20). By that he was saying that the New Covenant prophesied by Jeremiah was inaugurated by his death and resurrection, initiating an era in which God would write the law on people's hearts and make them his people, and all would know him from the greatest to the least (cf. Jeremiah 31:31-34, esp. vv. 33-34). Jesus is the source and dispenser of every blessing of the New Covenant—all we could ever hope and dream of.

Seventh, we come to forgiveness because of *sprinkled blood*: "to the sprinkled blood that speaks a better word than the blood of Abel." Abel's spilt blood cried condemnation and judgment from the ground, but Christ's blood shouts that we are forgiven and have peace with God.

Christians, the Scriptures tell us that in the church "you have come" (right now!) to these seven sublime realities: 1) to *the city of God*, 2) to *myriads of angels*, 3) to *fellow believers*, 4) to *God*, 5) to the *Church Triumphant*, 6) to *Jesus*, and 7) to *forgiveness*. No small thoughts here! If this does not create a wellspring of thanksgiving in your hearts and a longing for fellowship in the visible church, nothing will.

John Bunyan once told of falling into a despondency that lasted for several days and his desperately seeking a word from God to meet his need—and then this same grand text, Hebrews 12:22-24, came to him. Bunyan wrote:

> But that night was a good night to me; I have had but few better; I longed for the company of some of God's people, that I might have imparted unto them what God had showed me. Christ was a precious Christ to my soul that night; I could scarce lie in my bed for joy, and peace, and triumph through Christ.[3]

Hymn-writer John Newton wrote:

> *Savior, if of Zion's city,*
> *I through grace a member am,*
> *Let the world deride or pity,*
> *I will glory in Thy name.*

The dazzling images of the church assault us again and again throughout the New Testament in an effort to raise our thinking to the proper height—to deliver us from our small thoughts. As the church, we actually are Christ's *body* (Ephesians 1:22-23). We are a *temple* (Ephesians 2:19-22). We are the *bride* (Ephesians 5:25-33). We are his *sheep* (John 10:14-16, 25-30). We are the *branches* (John 15:5ff.). This should fill us with wonder and thanksgiving so that we sing, "I am his body, his temple, his bride, his sheep, his branch. I have come to his city—to angels—to firstborn coheirs—to God himself—to the Church Triumphant—to Jesus' new covenant—to forgiveness through his blood." No small thoughts!

These immense truths all tell us that the church will outlive the world. As Harry Blamires so eloquently observed:

> The world is like a great express train hurtling towards disaster—perhaps towards total destruction. And in this truly desperate situation certain passengers are running up and down the corridors announcing to each other that the Church is in great danger! The irony of it would be laughable if it were not so searing. Why, most of the Church's members have already got out at stations *en route*. And we ourselves shall be getting out soon anyway. And if the crash comes and the world is burnt to ashes, then the only thing that will survive the disaster will of course be the Church.[4]

Seen this way, in the clear light of biblical reality, the church is larger than the world itself. It is the enduring fact of our existence.

THE CHURCH: INDISPENSABLE

A cavalier disregard for the doctrine of the church is eccentric, to say the least. It disregards not only Scripture but also the consensus of the great thinkers throughout church history. Both Cyprian and Augustine could not conceive of salvation apart from the visible church. The Reformation doctors Luther and Calvin warned against those who neglect the visible church. And the Second Helvetic and Westminster Confessions said the same.[5]

The doctrine of the church ought to tell us that we are part of the grandest institution the universe has ever known, and that we are tragically diminished by nonparticipation in Christ's body.

Correspondingly, the church is diminished by our nonparticipation as well. *We need the church!* The Scriptures are most explicit regarding this: ". . . not neglecting to meet together, as is the habit of some, but encouraging one another, and all the more as you see the Day drawing near" (Hebrews 10:25). This straightforward exhortation ought to be enough in itself.

But there are also several other powerful reasons for faithful participation in the church, not the least of which is that, as Cyprian argued, we all need a mother. The church has certainly been that to me. It was the womb that warmed my soul until it was ready for birth when my pastor, Verl Lindley, led me to Christ. I was lovingly nurtured by the church through my youth group sponsors, Howard and Ruby Busse. In retrospect, I am in awe of how they allowed me and my buddies Dave and Jack to hang out in their home. The church gave me the milk of the Word through the strong teaching of my College Department teacher, Robert Seelye, who would begin the school year teaching Romans, and then the following year do the same. Robert "Romans" Seelye. The church saw me through hard times through the prayers of spiritual mothers like Roselva Taylor.

The church was the womb and cradle for my wife too— tiny Garfield Baptist on the west side of Long Beach, California. When our children came along, the church stood with us as we dedicated our children to God. She has also been the mother of my dearest friends. I owe so much to Christ's church—my life, my character, my worldview, my calling, my vision, my peace, my hope—everything.

Understanding, then, that we need the mothering of the church, we must also understand that we will never benefit from it as we should apart from commitment to its Head. The entire Christian life is about commitment—first and above all to Christ, but also to the church, to family, to marriage, to friendship, to ministry. None of these will ever flourish apart from commitment. Marriage, for example, can never produce the security, satisfaction, and growth that it promises unless there is commitment. On the most elementary level, you do not have to go to church to be a Christian. You do not have to go home to be married either. But in both cases if you do not, you will have a very poor relationship.

Here is the point: It is my considered belief that those who do not have the local church at the very center of their lives are likely not to make it as Christians through the opening decades of the third millennium. We are on the tide of unparalleled cultural change—exponential religious and ethical change. Very often those who live through a revolution do not know it. Most of you *do* know it. And you know that it is picking up speed—very much like the *Starship Enterprise* when it kicks into warp speed, even going to warp 10, so that whole galaxies fly by like fence posts.

Technology provides the metaphor to sense the deeper changes. Few think about it, but today's average consumers wear more computing power on their wrists than existed in the entire world before 1961. Many party games available in toy stores run on a higher-performance processor than the original 1976 Cray supercomputer, which in its day was accessible to only the most elite physicists. Microchips are doubling in performance every eighteen months.[6] In short, we are living in the middle of a technological tornado!

And all of this is only a shadow of the intellectual, social, ethical, and spiritual tides that are sweeping across our existence. Postmodernism is moving at gale force. The elites deny the existence of *any* universal truth or morality. Today we can no longer simply defend our faith as true; we must first defend the very *idea* of transcendent, universal truth. Postmodernists do not recognize truth, only preferences that are masks for the will to power. If truth as we see it is only our preferences driven by force, anything is possible.

Pluralism is also at high tide. The one thing that relativistic pluralism cannot tolerate is a person who believes that he/she has the truth. So if you claim to have the truth and you humbly insist that it is true for everyone, you're arrogant, you're to be watched, you're not good for society because your insistence that you are right is divisive. And the claim that Christ is the only way is particularly offensive.

Volcanic cultural changes lie ahead. The world as the young

know it today will be vastly different in fifteen years. And given the trajectory of philosophical, relativistic pluralism, it is sure to be less hospitable for the exclusive claims of historic Christianity.

This is why all who have determined to follow Christ desperately need the church. They need it for the things that it alone can supply in the precise ways that are needed, including the following:

• *The Word.* Nothing can replace the live preaching and teaching of the Word of God in the company of other like-minded believers. The combination of the Word opened by a preacher with a specific message to a specific congregation, plus the unique ministry of the Holy Spirit to those present in that corporate hour, are essential. As helpful as tapes can be, they cannot match or replace the live teaching of the Word to the congregation assembled as a whole or in classes and smaller groups.

• *Counsel.* The church also provides the example and counsel of more experienced, wiser believers. It is in the fellowship of the church that this ministry flourishes. This is what Christ's body is for. Its multiple gifts cause every part to grow. This does not happen in isolation.

• *Prayer.* The praying church is the church that empowers its people to stand tall. Remember Paul's injunction: ". . . praying at all times in the Spirit, with all prayer and supplication. To that end keep alert with all perseverance, making supplication for all the saints" (Ephesians 6:18-19).

• *A mother's nurture.* With God as your Father, the church will serve as your nurturing mother, providing a safe haven, an isle of sanity in a wild, confused world. This is why the local church must be at the center of your and your family's life—and why we must all devote ourselves to its ministry.

Hymn-writer Timothy Dwight expressed immortal truth when he wrote (1800) regarding the church:

> *For her my tears shall fall;*
> *For her my prayers ascend;*
> *To her my cares and toils be giv'n,*
> *Till toils and cares shall end.*

This said, there is something more that is necessary to counter the hostile winds of the new millennium, and that is the Lord's day.

THE LORD'S DAY: ESSENTIAL

The Lord's day is rooted in Israel's Sabbath as decreed in the fourth commandment, but it fulfills and supersedes it. Israel's Sabbath had come to them as a gracious gift of God when God rested from his work of creation (cf. Genesis 2:2-3). The Sabbath's distinctive was rest that commemorated the seven-day creational rhythm. The solar calendar is made of twelve lunar months, each having twenty-eight days, which gives us four seven-day phases. The Sabbath rides on these rhythms. Thus the Sabbath's purpose was to grace God's people—to grace their bodies with the rest of the Genesis rhythm—to grace their souls with heaven's rhythm, providing Israel with respite from their labors so they could focus on God and gratefully commemorate their liberation from bondage (cf. Deuteronomy 5:15). The Sabbath was both physically and spiritually beneficial.

But Jesus' resurrection brought forth a new day, "the first day" of the week, Sunday, which superseded the Sabbath. There is no doubt that Jesus rose from the grave on Sunday because there are references in all four Gospels to its occurring on "the first day" (cf. Matthew 28:1; Mark 16:1-2; Luke 24:1; John 20:1). Jesus memorialized the first day by appearing to his followers and breaking bread with them on the first day while on the road to Emmaus (cf. Luke 24:13-35). And then, one week later, Jesus appeared again on the first day to Thomas and the disciples (cf. John 20:26-29). Most significantly, the New Testament indicates that Christian worship was established on the first day (cf. Acts 20:7; 1 Corinthians 16:2). And by the time John wrote the book of Revelation, Sunday, the first day, had come to be called "the Lord's Day," as John records: "I was in the Spirit on the Lord's day" (Revelation 1:10).

From the beginning, the Lord's day, in contrast to the Sabbath, was not primarily a day of rest. It was a workday for most people. And because Christians had to work on that day, they met either early in the morning or in the evening after work. It was in such an evening meeting that poor Eutychus, tired after a day's work, fell out of a third-story window as Paul talked on into the night (cf. Acts 20:7-12). So we see from many sources that in the Christian church the Sabbath was superseded by the Lord's day. And more, we see that the great distinctive between the Sabbath and the Lord's day is this: Whereas the Sabbath distinctive is corporate *rest* in ceasing from labor, the Lord's day distinctive is corporate *worship* of the risen Lord.

This is a momentous distinction that has everything to do with our standing tall in the contrary currents of the new millennium. Here is why: Under the New Covenant, Christians are to worship all the time—in their individual lives, in their family lives, and when they come together for corporate worship. Corporate worship, then, is a particular expression of a life of perpetual worship. And in respect to this, weekly corporate worship on the Lord's day, Sunday, is meant to inform and enhance a life of worship the other six days of the week. The Christian's week begins with worship. Worship orders the week.

What happens to the church gathered on the Lord's day is mutual edification as we are built up together through corporate worship. Certainly we must study God's Word when we are alone. But there is added edification when we listen to it together and mutually assent to it and encourage one another to walk in it. It is also good to sing to God when we are alone. But how we are heartened when we joyously sing out amidst the many voices of corporate worship. We ought to affirm our credal beliefs when alone. But what courage we take in many voices roaring mutual affirmation—"I believe in God the Father Almighty . . ." And when we unite with each other in prayer, our hearts are taken to praises and petitions we would not have conceived on our own. When we come together corporately, we can encourage each other to a life of worship—to daily present our lives as burnt offerings to be consumed in God's service (cf. Romans 12:1-2).

When the writer of Hebrews gave his charge to Christians to join for corporate worship, he prefaced it by saying, "Let us hold fast the confession of our hope without wavering, for he who promised is faithful" (10:23). This is because the church was on the eve of the infamous Neronian persecution, when holding on to hope would be crucial. Then the writer added, "And let us consider how to stir up one another to love and good works" (v. 24). How would the church do this? ". . . not neglecting to meet together, as is the habit of some, but encouraging one another, and all the more as you see the Day drawing near" (v. 25).

The Scriptures contain no small thoughts about the church. Indeed, the church is the only thing that will survive the world's end. It is the enduring fact of our existence. Those who neglect the church do so to their own soul's detriment. Christians need to do the following:

• Resist the consumerist, hitchhiking mentality of our day and instead commit themselves to a local expression of Christ's body.

• Give themselves to building up the body of Christ with their prayers, time, service, and stewardship.

• Plan their lives and (if married) their family's lives around the life of the church instead of individual pursuits.

• Say no to sports programs and activities that take them away from church on the Lord's Day.

• Take care as to their television viewing and relaxation, so as not to erase the benefits of corporate worship.

• Love the church in a way that pleases Christ, who loved it and gave himself for it.

> *I love Thy kingdom, Lord,*
> *The house of Thine abode,*
> *The Church our blest Redeemer saved*
> *With His own precious blood.*

TIMOTHY DWIGHT, 1800

FOR REFLECTION AND APPLICATION

• How would you describe the place that the church has in the lives of most American Christians?

• Honestly assess the church's place in your own life.

• Have consumerism and individualism affected your attitude toward the church?

• In what ways might the church become more important to Christians in the years ahead?

• In light of scriptural teaching about the Lord's day, what changes might you make in your typical Sunday lifestyle?

NOTES

1. George Barna, *The Frog in the Kettle* (Ventura, CA: Regal Books, 1991), p. 133.

2. Origen, Homily on Luke 23:8, as quoted by Robert Louis Wilken, "Angels and Archangels: The Worship of Heaven and Earth," *Antiphon* 6:1 (2001): 10.

3. John Bunyan, *Grace Abounding to the Chief of Sinners* (Grand Rapids, MI: Zondervan, 1948), pp. 107-108.

4. Harry Blamires, *The Christian Mind* (Ann Arbor, MI: Servant, 1963), p. 153.

5. I have quoted Cyprian, Augustine, Luther, Calvin, and the Reformed confessions in my book *Disciplines of a Godly Man*, rev. ed. (Wheaton, IL: Crossway Books, 2001), pp. 170-171.

6. Price Pritchett, *New Work Habits for a Radically Changing World* (Dallas: Pritchett and Associates, n.d.), pp. 21, 25, 29, 37.

11

Set Apart to Save: The Unending Yes

The inspiration and motivation for this series came from the conjunction of two gripping revelations. The first was the appearance of a book by Robert Gundry with the daunting title *Jesus the Word According to John the Sectarian: A Paleofundamentalist Manifesto for Contemporary Evangelicalism, Especially Its Elites, in North America*—a title that I suspect the publisher (whose job it is to sell books) did not choose. This book, I hope, surprises everyone by gaining a large hearing.

Dr. Gundry's argument is that the instincts of early fundamentalism were right in their attempt to maintain theological orthodoxy and separation from the world, but that the movement was sidetracked by the fundamentalism of the twenties and forties into a shallow separatism. What is needed today is a new old fundamentalism that is in line with the paleofundamentalism of John's Gospel—a fundamentalism that while being in the world is morally separated from the world and that unashamedly preaches the Gospel. Professor Gundry states his concern in very specific terms:

> The "seeker sensitivity" of evangelicals—their practice of suiting the gospel to the felt needs of people, primarily the bourgeoisie— contributes to their numerical success but can easily sow the seeds of worldliness (broadly conceived). How so? Well, in a society such as ours where people do not feel particularly guilty before

God (though in fact they are), seeker-sensitivity—if consistently carried through—will soft-pedal the preaching of salvation from sin, for such preaching would not meet a felt need of people. As a result, the gospel *message* of saving, sanctifying grace reduces to a gospel *massage* of physical, psychological, and social well-being that allows worldliness to flourish.[1]

By worldliness Gundry means "not merely the disregard of fundamentalist taboos against smoking, drinking, dancing, movie-going, gambling and the like, but more expansively such matters as materialism, pleasure-seeking, indiscriminate enjoyment of salacious and violent entertainment, immodesty of dress, voyeurism, sexual laxity, and divorce."[2]

As this penetrating analysis gripped my heart (especially the incisive categories), the story of Lot's demise and degeneration came to me like a dual revelation. Here was a believer whom the New Testament three times calls "righteous" and who, though "distressed" by the sin of Sodom, hung on to Sodomite culture for dear life (cf. 2 Peter 2:7-8). Lot, in fact, had to be dragged from Sodom by the hand. And upon deliverance he made a whimpering plea with his angelic deliverers to go not to the hills but to the mini-Sodom of Zoar. From there he descended into a cave with his daughters and went down further in monumental degradation.

Tragically, Lot's Sodom-focused life had little positive effect on his wife and daughters. In fact, in the cave the culture of Sodom underwent a spiritual rebirth through the actions of Lot and his daughters. So we see that it is possible to be distressed by the world while hanging on to it for dear life! Indeed, Lot's life is paradigmatic of many of today's professing Christians who are at the same time both appalled and enthralled by the world. Gundry's categories provide an anatomy of evangelical enthrallment.

Together these two revelations "lit my fire" and fired my repeated calls to say no to materialism, and no to hedonism, and no to sensuality, and no to violence, and no to sexual sin, and no to immodesty, and no to divorce, and no to pluralism, and no to the marginalization of the church and the Gospel. The tenor of the passion of these noes ought to be on the level of the famous noes (the *neins!*) of Martin Niemoller and Dietrich Bonhoeffer to the theological and social excesses and aberrations of Weimar and Nazi Germany. We must say no—no farther, no more. If we do not take a stand, there will come a day when it is too late.

Now, this can all appear so grim. The call to the righteous can be seen as following the *via negativa*, the way of negation, the negative road. Faithfulness therefore becomes a gray, clenched-jaw, joyless, sour existence. But nothing could be farther from the eternal truth, or my intention for this book. These divinely ordained noes give birth to a life of affirmation—to an unending yes to the excellencies and benefactions of God. Here is a life that is openhanded, smiling, joyful, and good-natured. The set-apart life is not a dirge but a dance!

The Unending Yes

Materialism. Saying no to materialism sets us free from its gravitational pull and allows us to indulge in the yes of true riches. Many of us are weighed down by the delusive power of wealth into imagined supe-riorities and securities. The irrational, almost magical power of things exerts a god-like force that chokes the Word.

But the yes in the no to materialism opens us to God's riches right now—"And my God will supply every need of yours according to his riches in glory in Christ Jesus" (Philippians 4:19). The extent of God's provision? Every need we have. That's all! And the resources to do this? Christ's riches—the riches of the eternal Son. That's all! His riches are for the here and now. The benefits are joyous—a hilarity in giving that is irrational from the materialist's point of view, a sense of contentment and gain and an awareness of eternal investment.

The yes eventuates in truly unending riches, because you have actually laid up treasures in heaven that will not decay (cf. Matthew 6:19-21). The yes also lives in the unending reality that "in the com-ing ages" God will "show the immeasurable riches of his grace in kindness toward us in Christ Jesus" (Ephesians 2:7). In saying yes to the riches of Christ, we say yes to the things above—yes to being a coheir with Christ himself, yes to co-reigning with Christ, yes to a place prepared for us, yes to a crown! This yes will be substance for eternal song.

Hedonism. To pursue pleasures as an end in themselves is hedonistic folly; it is submitting to the tyranny of Huxley's *Brave New World*, where people are controlled by inflicting pleasure. But the yes in the no to hedonism opens us to the pleasures of God both earthly and heavenly. God has strewn his pleasures through all of life. Ironically, those who pursue them as entitlements miss them, but those who simply receive his ordained pleasures have them in full: pleasures of nature, pleasures of artistry, pleasures of family, pleasures of community, pleasures of worship. These pleasures can and ought to be more acute for believers because they alone are at peace with the Creator of all pleasures.

Transcending this is the grand hedonism of God himself—the unending pleasures of heaven that the Psalmist so memorably celebrates:

> *You make known to me the path of life;*
> *in your presence there is fullness of joy;*
> *at your right hand are pleasures forevermore.*
>
> —PSALM 16:11

Such is the eternal reality for every son and daughter of God. This yes has no end. Our life is to be a perpetual yes.

Sensuality. Saying no to viewing sensuality is an intensely spiritual matter because the television screen is the single most potent influence and control in western culture. The fact that Christians' viewing habits are virtually the same as general culture means that those under the thrall of the tube are having their sexuality desensitized, proselytized, and eroticized by prime-time lewdness and double entendre. At the same time, they are also being schooled in irreverence for God.

Here a no not only shuts off these degrading influences, but effects a yes to the sublime benefactions of God: "Finally, brothers, whatever is true, whatever is honorable, whatever is just, whatever is pure, whatever is lovely, whatever is commendable . . . think about these things" (Philippians 4:8). Every ingredient is positive. And our yes makes all the difference in the world. When we say yes to such excellencies, we are saying yes to the mind of Christ. The yes effects a song and a prayer that sets us apart to save:

May the mind of Christ my Savior
Live in me from day to day,
By His love and pow'r controlling
All I do and say.

KATE B. WILKINSON, 1925

Violence. The seventh Beatitude says, "Blessed are the peacemakers, for they shall be called sons of God" (Matthew 5:9), thus solemnizing Scripture's rejection of violent hearts. Indeed, God's Word uniformly pronounces an ominous woe to those who love violence— and by implication a woe upon the unparalleled factories of violence and voyeurism that exist in popular media that serve to desensitize and condition for violence.

A no to violence is, of course, a yes to the peace of Christ, who himself was long prophesied as the "Prince of Peace" (Isaiah 9:6), whose incarnation was greeted with angels' singing of peace on earth (Luke 2:14) and Simeon's oracle "Lord, now you are letting your servant depart in peace" (Luke 2:29). And finally, there was Christ's own declaration after his resurrection: "Peace I leave with you; my peace I give to you. Not as the world gives do I give to you" (John 14:27). A yes to his peace is a yes to unending *shalom*—and a life that is uniquely inviting in this conflict-ridden world.

Sexual conduct. Modern culture has taken the magnificent, multidimensional marital sexuality of the Bible and shrink-wrapped it into a flat-sided, single-dimensional, materialist package. Sex has become the mysticism of our materialist society, with its own sacred texts from D. H. Lawrence and his acolytes and its airbrushed media priests and priestesses. Our culture's landscape is littered with the throwaways of its sexual wreckage.

How refreshing, then, to say no to the sexual reductionism of cable TV and yes to the deep wells of Scripture as to our sexuality and relationships, with Christ at the very center. He provides the example and power to live under his blessing as sexual beings because he was not only incarnate, but is also the groom, and we the church are his bride. He has always been faithful to us. He has given his life for us. His goal is to present us to the Father without spot or blemish, holy and blameless. And he will do it. Jesus is our unending yes and sanctification. Such sanctification, such set-apartness, is essential in preaching the Gospel to the world.

Modesty. These are tough times for the modest. The cultural engines that fuel immodesty are immense: the fashion industry, the body industry, the beauty industry, and sin's own industry within our souls—all living off each other in dark symbiosis to promote an immodesty that at once demystifies, devalues, superficializes, tempts, and confuses.

To say no to immodesty is to embrace the incredible truth that we are made in God's image and, as such, are beautiful and unique creations of God—whether tall or short, skinny or unskinny, muscular or muscle-less. And more, we dress ourselves by putting on the apparel of God as Scripture repeatedly encourages us to do. Each putting on is a yes to God's adornment—beautiful eternal clothing that will know no end. To be so clothed by Christ sets us apart to powerfully minister the Word.

Pluralism. Today nothing will set you apart from culture more than saying no to the philosophical and theological pluralism that insists that objective truth cannot be known and that all religions are equally true. Yet that is what we must do in no uncertain terms. But the no is also a sublime yes to the Bible's explicit teaching about the exclusivity of Christ. The Old Testament rules out a smorgasbord of world religions. And the New Testament Gospels and epistles declare with one voice that Jesus is the only way to God and that all are lost apart from him. Jesus is the only way. If there was another way, he would not have died on the cross!

Our unending yes already has its eternal lyrics:

> *"Worthy is the Lamb who was slain, to receive power and wealth and wisdom and might and honor and glory and blessing!"*
> —REVELATION 5:12

And it is this mighty yes that propels us to take the Gospel to the ends of the earth!

Marriage. A 25 percent marital holocaust of divorce has descended on the church and culture to the extent that there is no difference statistically between Christians and non-Christians. Here there must be a resounding no to those things that undermine marriage, the antinomianism that ignores God's Word, narcissism's "me first" self-love, and hedonism's acid reign of pleasure. And this resounding no must then be countered by a mighty yes in our marriages—first to the *cross*, affirming that Christ is the center of our marriage and that husbands and wives will die for each other, then affirming that our marriage *covenant* is for life and that we will never ever break it, and then affirming that husbands and wives are both "in *Christ,*" the bridegroom who is at the center of our marriages. We must say yes to the cross, the covenant, and the Christ if we are to be set apart to save.

The church. The Scriptures contain no small thoughts about the church. In truth, the church is the only thing that will survive the world's end. That is the enduring fact of our existence. When we come to the church, we say yes to the city of God, yes to angels, yes to coheirs, yes to God, yes to the Church Triumphant, yes to Jesus, yes to forgiveness (cf. Hebrews 12:22-24). We also say yes to meeting together, yes to the Lord's day, yes to commitment, yes to loving the church in a way that pleases Christ who loved it and gave himself for it. The yes is unending because the church is without end.

The Gospel. When we exposit Paul's declaration of the Gospel— "that Christ died for our sins in accordance with the Scriptures, that he was buried, that he was raised on the third day in accordance with the

Scriptures" (1 Corinthians 15:3-4)—we understand that everything in our salvation is from God. We say yes to the wonderful truth that our salvation was God-conceived, God-motivated, God-generated, God-finished, and God-bestowed. The Gospel as Paul says in the opening verse of Romans is "the gospel of God." It is his story, *Godspell*, God's story. He is the creator and consummator of our salvation.

> *"Salvation belongs to our God who sits on the throne, and to the Lamb!"*
>
> —REVELATION 7:10

So we see in all of this that the divinely ordained noes give birth to a life of affirmation—an unending yes to the excellencies and benefactions of God. The no to materialism is a yes to the riches of God. The no to hedonism is a yes to the pleasures of God on earth and in heaven. The no to sensual fixations is a yes to the mind of Christ. The no to violence is a yes to the peace of Christ. The no to the reductionist view of sexuality is a yes to the deep wells of Scripture that place Christ at the very center of life. The no to immodesty is a joyous yes to the image of God and the clothing he provides. The no to pluralism is a yes to Christ as the way, the truth, and the life—the only way to God. The no to divorce is a yes to marriage and the cross and the covenant and Christ. When we say no to self and individualism, we say yes to the church and the dizzying excellencies of Zion. When we say no to saving ourselves and yes to the Gospel, we receive a salvation that is all of God. "He who did not spare his own Son but gave him up for us all, how will he not also with him graciously give us all things?" (Romans 8:32).

TO SAVE

As we have emphasized throughout, there is no power in the no. The no by itself is mere moralism. A people set apart merely by the noes have no power. Such are very much like the world's religions. The power is in the yes because all the yeses are yeses to Christ: yes to his riches, yes to his pleasures, yes to his mind, yes to his peace, yes to his relationship, yes to his clothing, yes to the cross and the covenant and Christ, yes to him as the only way, yes to his body the church, and yes to the Gospel of God.

People who live in this yes will not succumb to Lot's folly of being both appalled and enthralled by the world. They will be set apart to Christ—that is, *set apart to save.* Like Christ, distinct from the world, they will be in a position to minister the Gospel to the world. Instead of assimilation, they will live in mission.

God's original intention for his people was that they reach out to the world, as was stated in his promise to Abram that he would make him a blessing and that all the peoples of the earth would be blessed through him (cf. Genesis 12:2-3). Abraham himself failed in this, as, for example, in his pathetic testimony to the Canaanite King Abimelech (cf. Genesis 20). Some four hundred years later, at Sinai, at the giving of the law, God instructed Moses to say to Israel:

> *"You yourselves have seen what I did to the Egyptians, and how I bore you on eagles' wings and brought you to myself. Now therefore, if you will indeed obey my voice and keep my covenant, you shall be my treasured possession among all peoples, for all the earth is mine; and you shall be to me a kingdom of priests and a holy nation. These are the words that you shall speak to the people of Israel."*
>
> —EXODUS 19:4-6

Again, though Israel did well at times, they failed as a people both to maintain holiness and to become a kingdom of priests.

But gloriously, when Christ came as the ultimate seed of Abraham (cf. Galatians 3:8, 16, 29) and of true Israel (cf. Matthew 2:15), he fulfilled everything by his perfect holiness and eternal priesthood (Matthew 4:1-11; Luke 4:1-13) and by becoming a light to the Gentiles (cf. Luke 2:32; John 8:12). In the New Covenant, those of us who are "in Christ" are duty-bound and empowered to fulfill the age-old calling of Israel to be "a chosen race, a royal priesthood, a holy nation, a people for his own possession, that you may proclaim the excellencies of him who called you out of darkness into his marvelous light" (1 Peter 2:9). Brothers and sisters, "His divine power has granted to us all things that pertain to life and godliness, through the knowledge of him who called us to his own glory and excellence" (2 Peter 1:3).

We must say yes to him, and yes to his call to reach our lost world.

NOTES

1. Robert H. Gundry, *Jesus the Word According to John the Sectarian: A Paleofundamentalist Manifesto for Contemporary Evangelicalism, Especially Its Elites, in North America* (Grand Rapids, MI: Eerdmans, 2002), pp. 77-78.
2. Ibid., p. 77.

Appendix: I

The Gospel—Old and New

How amazing. How wonderful the Gospel is. But the common wonder of our gospel experience harbors an irony, which is this: Many people who have been saved by the Gospel cannot explain what the Gospel is! Invariably when a group of Christians are asked to define the Gospel, they find themselves stretched. Some describe its benefits. Some list essential gospel passages like John's belief texts or "the Romans Road." Others may describe techniques for sharing the Gospel or an outline of gospel truth. These are all good things and are helpful in sharing the Gospel. But very few can define the Gospel biblically. And this is not just a problem with the people in the pew. Many seminary students experience the same difficulties.

Similarly, many Christians when asked how they know they are Christians answer, "Because I accepted Christ" or "Because I prayed" or "Because I went forward." Notice the recurrence of "I"? All of these answers give prominence to what the person has done, whereas the Gospel is about what God has done.

In the religious marketplace of many gospels (social gospels, therapeutic gospels, political gospels, man-centered gospels), it is of marked importance to be able to know and explain what the Gospel is. Christians who are set apart by knowing and owning the biblical Gospel will be positioned to weather the religious free-for-all that swirls around the Gospel.

SET APART BY OUR UNDERSTANDING OF THE GOSPEL

Significantly the English word *gospel* is derived from the Anglo-Saxon *Godspell*, "God Story," used to translate the Greek *euangelion*, "good news." The sense of "God Story" bears witness to the New Testament use of *Gospel* to sum up the fact that Christ is the fulfillment of the Old Testament Scriptures. The Gospel as God Story is what the Old Testament is about. Thus the Gospel is not new with the New Testament but is as old as the Old Testament. The God Story is rooted in earliest revelation. Paul called it "the gospel of God" in the opening verse of Romans.

The Gospel Is Old

Paul stated explicitly that the essentials of the Gospel came out of the Old Testament Scriptures:

> *Now I would remind you, brothers, of the gospel I preached to you, which you received, in which you stand, and by which you are being saved, if you hold fast to the word I preached to you—unless you believed in vain. For I delivered to you as of first importance what I also received: that* Christ [Messiah] died for our sins *in accordance with the Scriptures, that he was buried, that* he was raised on the third day *in accordance with the Scriptures.*
>
> —1 CORINTHIANS 15:1-4, EMPHASIS ADDED

Whenever Paul preached the Gospel, he preached at least two things: 1) that the Christ (Messiah) died as was spelled out in the Old Testament Scriptures, and 2) that he likewise was resurrected as detailed in the Old Testament.

Messiah's death. Plainly the Old Testament revealed the Messiah's death with a progressive intensity. Early on, the Old Covenant was launched in a sea of blood from sacrificial animals as described in Exodus 24. And the sacrificial system that followed perpetuated the death of innocent animals to effect ceremonial cleansing of the offerers. The daily sacrifices pointed to and called for the ultimate atoning sacrificial death of Christ.

In a similar way the Passover lamb of Exodus 12 had prophesied of Christ's sufferings and death. The Passover lamb had to be a male in his prime without defect (cf. Exodus 12:5), and none of his bones could be broken in the sacrificial process (12:46)—all true of Messiah. And most of all, the blood of the Passover lamb shielded the faithful Israelites from death (12:13, 22-23). Christ would fulfill these details to the letter. Christ, in fact, identified himself as the Passover lamb (cf. Luke 22:15-16; cf. 1 Corinthians 5:7).

The entire tabernacle spoke of Christ, and the epicenter of the tabernacle (the mercy seat atop the Ark of the Covenant where the blood was sprinkled) pictured Christ's atoning/propitiating work. In fact, the New Testament word "propitiation" comes from the root word for mercy seat, so that the apostle John would explain of Christ, "He is the propitiation for our sins, and not for ours only but also for the sins of the whole world" (1 John 2:2; cf. Romans 3:25). By his death Jesus became the atoning place and atoning blood for our sins.

Later the prophetic Scriptures in Isaiah 53 were very explicit about Christ's sufferings. In fact, Christ himself in the Upper Room would direct his disciples to Isaiah 53 by quoting its final verse, indicating that he himself "'was numbered with the transgressors,'" thus alerting them to the fact that every line of Isaiah 53 referred to him (Luke 22:37; cf. Isaiah 53:12b).

And then, of course, Psalm 22 gives a technical description of a man dying by crucifixion before death on a cross had been invented! Jesus' quotation of the opening line of that Psalm from the cross in the hour before his death on the cross sealed its prophetic application to him alone. "In effect," he says, "read Psalm 22. It's about me, in every detail." Thus Paul's Gospel-claim that "Christ died for our sins in accordance with the Scriptures" (1 Corinthians 15:3) was and is substantiated in profound detail in the whole range of the Old Testament.

Messiah's resurrection. Likewise Paul's other gospel essential, that Christ "was raised on the third day in accordance with the Scriptures" (1 Corinthians 15:4), also accords with the progressive revelation of the Old Testament Scriptures. The idea of a resurrection was intimated in Abraham's comment to his servant as he took Isaac up the

mount with the intention of sacrificing him: "Stay here with the don-
key; I and the boy will go over there and worship [meaning Isaac's
sacrifice] and come again to you [because God will raise him up]"
(Genesis 22:5). My imaginative interpretation? Not according to the
writer of Hebrews, who says of this:

> By faith Abraham, when he was tested, offered up Isaac, and he who
> had received the promises was in the act of offering up his only son, of
> whom it was said, "Through Isaac shall your offspring be named." He
> considered that God was able even to raise him from the dead, from
> which, figuratively speaking, he did receive him back.
>
> —11:17-19

There was also an intimation of resurrection in God's famous
declaration to Moses at the burning bush in Exodus 3:6: "I am the
God of your father, the God of Abraham, the God of Isaac, and the
God of Jacob." Jesus used this text to embarrass some resurrection-
denying Sadducees by pointing out that God's use of the present
tense—"I am the God of. . ."—indicates that the deceased patriarchs
were alive; otherwise he wouldn't have used the present tense, but
rather the past—"I was" (Luke 20:37-38; cf. Acts 3:13-15).

As to the resurrection of Christ himself, the apostle Peter
explained in his sermon at Pentecost that Psalm 16 prophesied
Christ's resurrection. His reasoning was that David's words—
"Therefore my heart is glad, and my whole being rejoices; my flesh
also dwells secure. For you will not abandon my soul to Sheol, or let
your holy one see corruption" (Psalm 16:9-10)—did not refer to
himself, but to his ultimate Son who rose from the dead before bod-
ily decomposition began. Peter's words left no doubt as he said:

> "Brothers, I may say to you with confidence about the patriarch David
> that he both died and was buried, and his tomb is with us to this day.
> Being therefore a prophet, and knowing that God had sworn with an
> oath to him that he would set one of his descendants on his throne, he
> foresaw and spoke about the resurrection of the Christ, that he was not

abandoned to Hades, nor did his flesh see corruption. This Jesus God raised up, and of that we all are witnesses."

—ACTS 2:29-32

Finally, as to Paul's insistence that Christ "was raised on the third day in accordance with the Scriptures" (1 Corinthians 15:4), it must first be noted that this accords with Christ's own words of explanation on the night of his resurrection when he told his disciples, "Thus it is written, that the Christ should suffer and on the third day rise from the dead" (Luke 24:46). And where in the Old Testament is the third day that Christ referenced? Christ was alluding to Hosea 6:2: "After two days he will revive us; on the third day he will raise us up, that we may live before him." That prophecy was given to sinful Israel, but there was nothing in their history to correspond to it, except that when Christ rose from the dead on the third day, he raised with himself believing Israel (cf. Galatians 3:29; 6:16).

So we see that the good news of the Gospel is *Godspell*, "God Story." Salvation through Messiah's death and resurrection was his plan from the beginning. It was planned before the world began (cf. Revelation 13:8). It was, and is, all of God.

The Gospel Is New

As we come to the New Testament, everything rides on the death and resurrection of Christ. All the promises of Scripture are "Yes in him" (2 Corinthians 1:20).

Christ's death on the cross answered the problem of our sin. On the cross he became sin for us (2 Corinthians 5:21). All of our sins were poured out on his righteous person. There he died for our sins. He paid the price in full. He could do it because he was both divine and human.

Then as we trusted in him, he gave us his righteousness. "For our sake he made him to be sin who knew no sin, so that in him we might become the righteousness of God" (2 Corinthians 5:21).

This is a grand theme of the book of Romans. Notice the relation of faith and righteousness in the following texts:

For in it the righteousness *of God is revealed from* faith *for* faith, *as it is written, "The* righteous *shall live by* faith. *"*
— ROMANS 1:17, EMPHASIS ADDED

God's own righteousness is given to those who trust in him.

. . . *the* righteousness *of God through* faith *in Jesus Christ for all who* believe.
— ROMANS 3:22, EMPHASIS ADDED

For we hold that one is justified by faith *apart from works of the law.*
— ROMANS 3:28, EMPHASIS ADDED

. . . *and be found in him, not having a* righteousness *of my own that comes from the law, but that which comes through* faith *in Christ, the* righteousness *from God that depends on* faith.
— PHILIPPIANS 3:9, EMPHASIS ADDED

Those who would be saved are called to belief in Christ.

But to all who did receive him, who believed *in his name, he gave the right to become children of God.*
— JOHN 1:12, EMPHASIS ADDED

For God so loved the world, that he gave his only Son, that whoever believes *in him should not perish but have eternal life.*
— JOHN 3:16, EMPHASIS ADDED

"Truly, truly, I say to you, whoever hears my word and believes *him who sent me has eternal life. He does not come into judgment, but has passed from death to life."*
— JOHN 5:24, EMPHASIS ADDED

Then they said to him, "What must we do, to be doing the works of God?" Jesus answered them, "This is the work of God, that you believe *in him whom he has sent."*
— JOHN 6:28-29, EMPHASIS ADDED

Does the Gospel work? As surely as Christ was raised from the dead! Paul's great declaration of the Gospel through Christ's death and resurrection in 1 Corinthians 15:1-4 is followed by his assurance of the resurrection:

> . . . *he appeared to Cephas, then to the twelve. Then he appeared to more than five hundred brothers at one time, most of whom are still alive, though some have fallen asleep. Then he appeared to James, then to all the apostles. Last of all, as to one untimely born, he appeared also to me.*
>
> —1 CORINTHIANS 15:5-8

Paul goes on to say that if there is no resurrection, we are a pitiful lot.

> *And if Christ has not been raised, then our preaching is in vain and your faith is in vain. We are even found to be misrepresenting God, because we testified about God that he raised Christ, whom he did not raise if it is true that the dead are not raised. For if the dead are not raised, not even Christ has been raised. And if Christ has not been raised, your faith is futile and you are still in your sins. Then those also who have fallen asleep in Christ have perished. If in this life only we have hoped in Christ, we are of all people most to be pitied.*
>
> —VV. 14-19

If Christ was not resurrected, we're the crew on a ship of fools. However, if the Messiah has been resurrected, we are blessed beyond human words. The divine power that propelled Christ from the grave victorious over sin and death has borne our sins away, and we share in the resurrection right now (cf. Romans 6:1-11).

Christians, followers of Christ, everything is from God. Our salvation was God-conceived, God-motivated, God-generated, God-finished, and God-bestowed. Again as Paul says in the opening verse of Romans, the Good News is "the gospel of God" (Romans 1:1). It is his story—Godspell. He is the creator and consummator of our salvation. That is why when we are asked about our salvation, the pronoun I is inappropriate. It is always, "Because God . . ." or "Because Christ . . ." In these confused days, we must set ourselves apart in our understanding of the Gospel. Everything is from him, and all glory goes to him.

SET APART BECAUSE OF OUR DEVOTION TO THE GOSPEL

And ultimately, because we are set apart in our *understanding* of the Gospel, we must be set apart in our *devotion* to the Gospel. We must call out with Paul, "For I am not ashamed of the gospel, for it is the power of God for salvation to everyone who believes, to the Jew first and also to the Greek" (Romans 1:16). Through the death and resurrection of his Son, God reached down to Paul, a persecutor of Christ and his church, and saved him. Through Christ's death and resurrection, God has reached down to us and has given us life.

The Gospel must be our center. The Gospel must be our song. *Godspell*, the God Story rooted in all the Scriptures, must be our passion. Such power here! It brings life and forgiveness and relationship and peace and understanding and mercy and love and mission.

This is the best news ever proclaimed. There will never be better news in all the universe—ever! "Blessed be the God and Father of our Lord Jesus Christ, who has blessed us in Christ with every spiritual blessing in the heavenly places" (Ephesians 1:3).

Apart from the Gospel, all our efforts to set ourselves apart so that we might minister to the world are futile. Apart from the Gospel our effort to forego materialism, to reject hedonism, to avoid viewing sensuality and violence, to be pure, to be modest, to cultivate marriage, to love the church and celebrate the Lord's day—all these efforts are mere moralism. So what if we do these things! There is no power in them. Moralism never saved a soul. Only the Gospel saves.

Yet if Christ is the center of our lives, if our riches are in him, if our pleasures come from him, if he controls our viewing habits, if he is the Lord of our sexuality, if he informs our modesty, if he is the center of our marriage, if he is Lord of his day—and if with all of this the Gospel is lived and declared, there will be *power*.

The Gospel is this: "For I delivered to you as of first importance what I also received: that Christ died for our sins in accordance with the Scriptures, that he was buried, that he was raised on the third day in accordance with the Scriptures" (1 Corinthians 15:3-4). He has done everything!

All you have to do is come believing, just as you are. There is a proper place for the personal pronouns I and you, if you are coming to Christ believing in his finished work. Your prayer and your coming must be:

Just as I am, without one plea,
But that thy blood was shed for me,
And that thou bidd'st me come to Thee,
O Lamb of God, I come, I come.

CHARLOTTE ELLIOTT, 1834

Appendix: II

Internet Safety

WEBSITES FOR MOVIE REVIEWS

Christian Sites

Christianity Today Film Forum: www.ChristianityToday.com/ctmag/features/columns/film forum.html. Summarizes what Christian reviewers are saying; has links to other sites.

ChristianSpotlight.com: www.christiananswers.net/spotlight/movies rating. Criteria: Excellent, Good (nothing offensive), Better Than Average (slightly objectionable), Average (somewhat offensive), Very Offensive, Extremely Offensive. Includes compilations of movie lists that you can view by "Moral Rating."

Focus on the Family Plugged In: www.family.org/pplace/pi. Comprehensive resource on film, music, and TV reviews from a Christian perspective.

Secular Sites

www.screenit.com—reviews movies and music. Criteria: Alcohol/Drugs, Blood/Gore, Disrespectful/Bad Attitude, Frightening Tense Scenes, Guns/Weapons, Imitative Behavior, Jump Scenes, Music (scary/tense), Music (inappropriate), Profanity, Sex/Nudity, Smoking, Tense Family Scenes, Topics to Talk About, Violence.

www.dove.org: Criteria: Sex, language, violence, nudity, drugs, alcohol. Rating color chart.

www.FamilyCow.com: Criteria: Entertainment value, acceptability, film with acceptable elements, film with objectionable elements.

INTERNET FILTERS

www.filterreview.com
www.familyclick.com
www.software4parents.com
www.familyconnect.com/trial/default.asp?RN=r3098

A number of available Internet filters do a good job of building a firewall for your family. I know of a family in which the father sits down with his boys weekly and reviews the websites they have visited.

INTERNET SAFETY TIPS

Check out www.christianitytoday.com/kids/features/parents.html for helpful pointers. In addition, consider the following.

Invest in positive resources. Anticipating the question of what to do when TV is dethroned, Bob DeMoss answers:

> You can read as many newspapers and magazines as you like. You may listen to radio. Play board or card games. Enjoy music. Play a computer game—including the responsible use of Gameboy. Get lost in a book. Use the Internet. Savor long walks. Linger at the dinner table for conversation and storytelling. Study your Bible. Engage in sports. Finish a project. Start a puzzle. Introduce yourself to a neighbor. Take a night course. Go swimming. Make a model airplane. Take a drive in the country. Even bungee jump. Fly a kite. Or write the next great novel.[1]

Groucho Marx once said, "I find television very educational. Every time someone switches it on I go into another room and read a book."[2]

This is all true. But it requires investing in some family resources, such as the following:

• *Videos/DVDs.* Wisdom dictates that if you're going to toss *some* videos, you ought to build a library of excellent films. Barbara and I have done this for ourselves and with an eye to our grandchildren. We have even put together a recommended list.

• *Music.* Build a rich music library and invest in good components. Careful shopping will in a short time accrue amazing resources.

• *Books on tape.* You will be amazed at the excellent titles available in the big bookstores. Listening to a great book well-read is almost always more gripping than its cinematic rendering.

• *Books.* Fill your home with great books for every age. My wife has always had an eye out for children's books for all ages and has accumulated exciting resources in our home—especially now for our grandchildren.

• *Library.* Your local library has astounding resources, and perhaps your church library as well (the library in the church I pastor has twelve thousand books, seven hundred videos, and two hundred audiotapes plus most of the Christian periodicals).

NOTES

1.   Bob DeMoss, Jr., *TV The Great Escape* (Wheaton, IL: Crossway Books, 2001), p. 43.
2.   Ibid., p. 21.

Scripture Index

General Index